THE STORY OF LINCOLN
(An Introduction to the History of the City)

by
E. I. ABELL
and
J. D. CHAMBERS, Ph.D.

With a new Introduction
by
Sir Francis Hill

Republished by S.R. Publishers Ltd., 1971
from the second (1949) edition (Revised)
First published by the City of Lincoln Education Committee, 1939

Bibliography

Hill, J. W. F. *Medieval Lincoln*. Cambridge University Press 1948
Hill, J. W. F. *Tudor and Stuart Lincoln*. C.U.P. 1956
Hill, Sir Francis. *Georgian Lincoln*. C.U.P. 1966

Reproduced 1971 by S.R. Publishers Limited,
East Ardsley, Wakefield,
Yorkshire, England
by kind permission of the
copyright holder

ISBN 0 85409 713 9

Please address all enquiries to S.R. Publishers Ltd.
(address as above)

Reprinted by Scolar Press Ltd.,
Menston, Yorkshire, U.K.

THE STORY OF LINCOLN
(An Introduction to the History of the City)

INTRODUCTION

This book is the product of a happy cooperation between two very different men. Ernest Israel Abell, who was born in Lincoln in 1890, served for 40 years as a teacher of history in schools in Lincoln. He was an enthusiastic local historian and antiquary, and for many years held office as secretary of the Lincoln Historical Association. He compiled a series of scrapbooks, gathered from a variety of sources, on the history of Lincoln. In the first instance he did this for his own pleasure, but he soon discovered the value of local history in making more vivid his history teaching in school; and so his collections became widely known and admired.

Jonathan David Chambers was born in 1898 at Eastwood, Nottinghamshire, and he became a student at University College Nottingham. He taught in the University Department of Adult Education, and after working in a school during the Second World War, returned to the University, in which in 1959 he became Professor of Economic History, the first to hold that title. He became one of the most eminent scholars in his field.

Both men readily responded to suggestions first made by Mr C. W. Hooton, Director of Education for the city of Lincoln (1931-1948) that they should jointly produce a history of Lincoln for schools, and the Lincoln Education Committee undertook its publication. Ernest Abell provided most of the material, and David Chambers did most of the writing. The book appeared in 1939.

For some years the book has been out of print. The need for such a work has been much felt, and after consideration the Lincoln Education Committee decided that they could not do better than reprint it, making such corrections and additions as time and research had made necessary.

It will give pleasure to the many friends of two much loved men that this memorial to them should be thus renewed.

Francis Hill

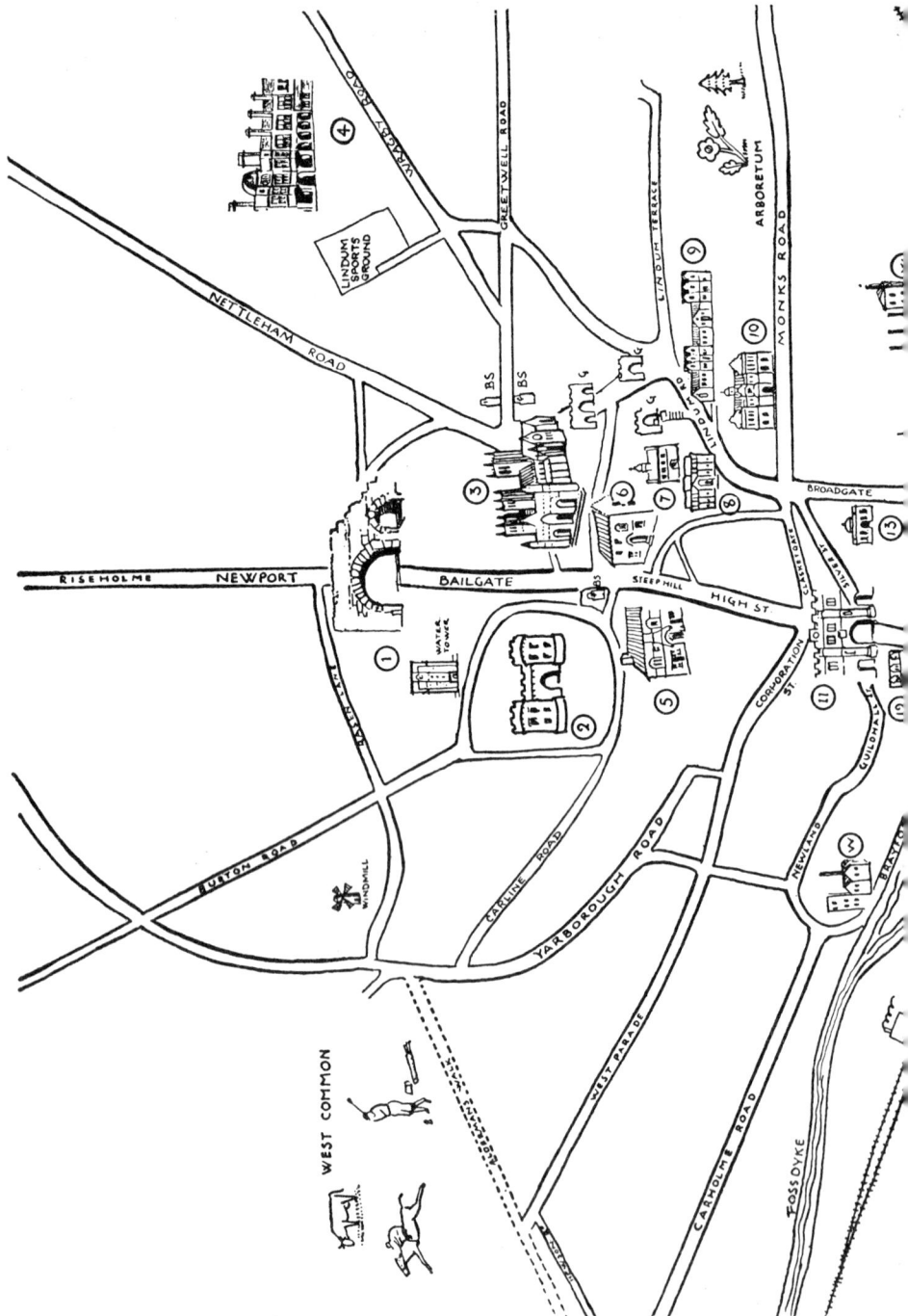

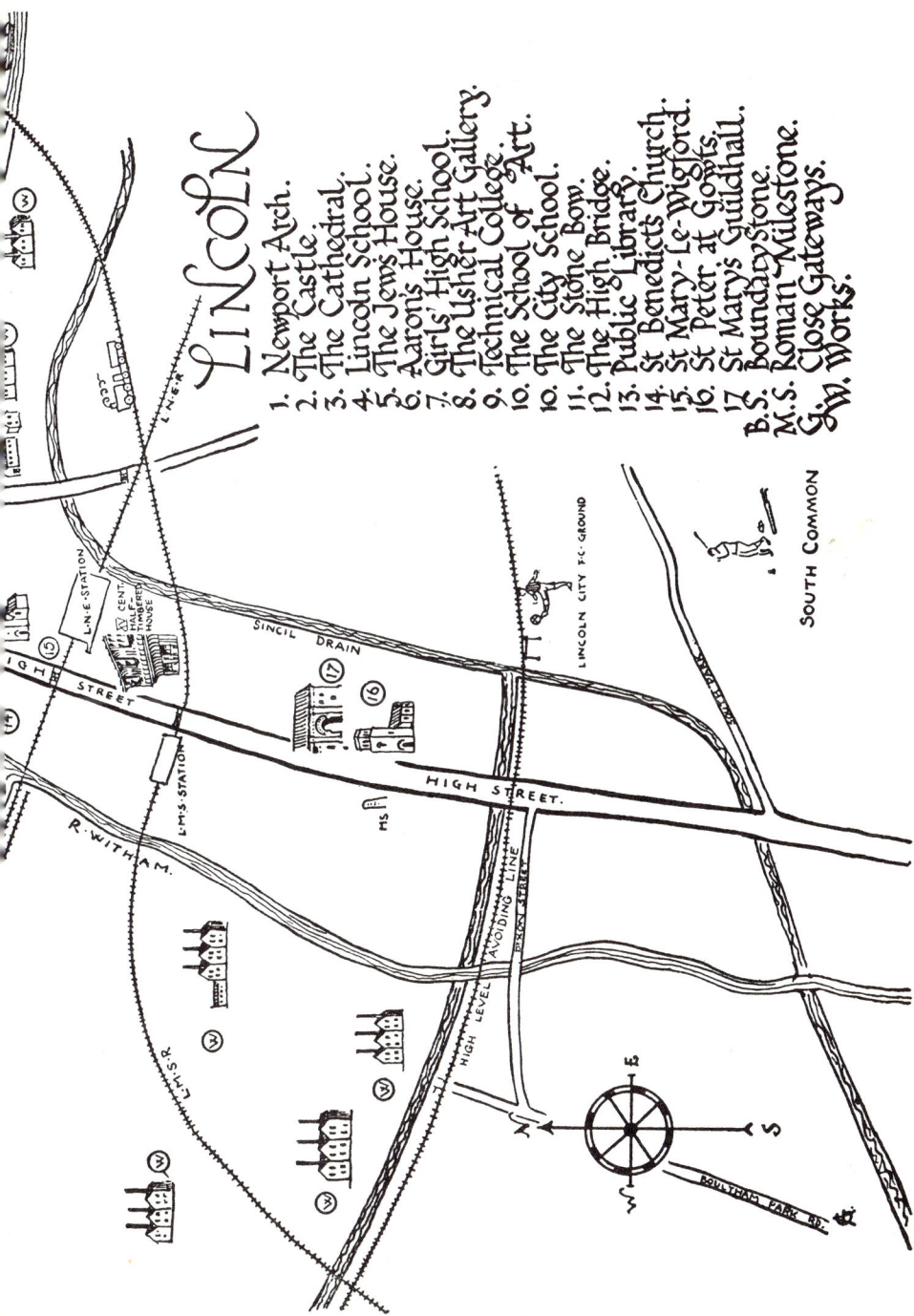

LINCOLN

1. Newport Arch.
2. The Castle.
3. The Cathedral.
4. Lincoln School.
5. The Jews House.
6. Aaron's House.
7. Girls' High School.
8. The Usher Art Gallery.
9. Technical College.
10. The School of Art.
10. The City School.
11. The Stone Bow.
12. The High Bridge.
13. Public Library.
14. St Benedict's Church.
15. St Mary-Le-Wigford.
16. St Peter at Gowts.
17. St Mary's Guildhall.
B.S. Boundary Stone.
M.S. Roman Milestone.
G. Close Gateways.
W. Works.

SOUTH COMMON

SINCIL DRAIN

LINCOLN CITY F.C. GROUND

HIGH STREET.

HIGH LEVEL AVOIDING LINE

PELHAM STREET

R. WITHAM.

L.M.S. STATION

L.N.E. STATION

CENT.
HALF-TIMBERED HOUSE

HIGH STREET

L.N.E.R.

L.M.S.R.

BOULTHAM PARK RD.

M.S.

HIGH STREET
(From a painting dated 1843 by W. Callow)

THE STORY OF LINCOLN

(AN INTRODUCTION TO THE HISTORY OF THE CITY)

BY

E. I. ABELL
Rosemary School, Lincoln

AND

J. D. CHAMBERS, Ph.D.
University College, Nottingham
(*Author of "Nottingham in the 18th Century," etc.*)

WITH LINE DRAWINGS BY
AUSTIN GARLAND AND HERBERT STEADMAN

PUBLISHED BY
THE CITY OF LINCOLN EDUCATION COMMITTEE

First Published July, 1939

Second Edition (Revised), March, 1949

PRINTED IN GREAT BRITAIN BY KEYWORTH AND SONS
SWANPOOL COURT, LINCOLN

CONTENTS.

CHAPTER		PAGE
	Foreword	7
I	Looking Backwards—The Trackway—The Site	9
II	Roman Lincoln—Approach—Lindum from the North—From inside—Plan of City—Engineering works—Lindum from the South	15
III	Saxon and Danish Lincoln	27
IV	Norman Lincoln	35
V	Famous Bishops	44
VI	Red Letter Days	54
VII	Lincoln in the Middle Ages—How Lincoln was governed ...	70
VIII	The Jews in Lincoln	77
IX	Lincoln and the Wool Trade	85
X	The Gilds—The Craft Gilds—The Weavers' Gild—Later Gilds—Religious side of Gilds	88
XI	Markets and Fairs	97
XII	Religious Houses—Monks' Abbey—St. Catherine's—The Friars — The Franciscans — The Dominicans — The Hospitals—The Malandry—The Holy Sepulchre—St. Giles'—St. Bartholomew's—St. Leonard's ...	103
XIII	Days of Decline	121
XIV	Period of Reformation—Lincolnshire Rebellion—Religious Persecution	124
XV	The Reformation and the Churches—The Chantries—High Bridge Chapel	130
XVI	The Civil Wars	137
XVII	The Rise of Nonconformity	147
XVIII	Education—Grammar School—Bluecoat School ...	153
XIX	Social Problems—Poor Law—Highways—Law and Order—Prisons	160
XX	The Coming of Democracy—The Bail—The Close—Beaumont Fee	167
XXI	The Rise of Modern Lincoln—Enclosures—Enclosure of Lincoln—Transport—The Coming of the Railways—Growth of Modern Industry	187
XXII	Modern Lincoln—Housing—Water—Fire Fighting Services —Gas and Electricity—Public Transport—The Corporation—Two great Enterprises—Industry after the Great War	204
XXIII	War Returns to Lincoln	214
	The Castle	218
	The Cathedral	222
	Ancient Gatehouses	224
	List of Authorities	229
	Index	235

ILLUSTRATIONS

Plates

High Street (W. Callow)	.. .. ..	Frontispiece	
Newport Arch	.. ..	Opposite page	16
Little Bargate	.. ..	,, ,,	32
The Jews' House and Jews' Court	.. ..	,, ,,	64
The High Bridge ..	.. ..	,, ,,	80
St. Mary's Guildhall	.. ..	,, ,,	96
The Cathedral and Old St. Paul's Church	..	,, ,,	112
The Cathedral Chapter House ..	.. ..	,, ,,	128
St. Peter-at-Arches Church	.. .. ..	,, ,,	144
High Street (A. C. Pugin)	.. .. ..	,, ,,	160
The Stonebow	.. ..	,, ,,	192
The Castle	.. ..	,, ,,	208

Line Drawings

Tombstone of a Standard Bearer of the Ninth Legion	..	Page	15
Tombstone of Gaius Julius Galenus	.. .. ..	,,	16
Roman Milestone found in Bailgate	.. ..	,,	20
Roman Milestone found at the Western end of Sibthorp Street	.. ..	,,	24
Part of a Roman Milestone ..	.. .. ..	,,	25
Old St. Martin's Church	.. ..	,,	29
Danish Comb Case found at Lincoln	.. ..	,,	30
Great Bargate ..	.. ..	,,	32
Newland Gate ..	.. ..	,,	33
Figure on the Cathedral showing Medieval Costume	..	,,	40
West Front of the Norman Cathedral	.. ..	,,	45
Tomb of Remigius	.. ..	,,	47
Statue on Cathedral said to represent St. Hugh	..	,,	50
Clasketgate	.. ..	,,	56
Remains of John of Gaunt's Palace ..	.. ..	,,	57
Statues of Edward I and Eleanor	.. .. ..	,,	59
Chair in the Chapter House (without modern canopy)	..	,,	61
Sword of Richard II ..	.. ..	,,	63
Plan of Bishop's Palace	.. ..	,,	65
Figure on the Cathedral showing Medieval Costume	..	,,	72

Illustrations—*continued*

The House of Aaron .. .. Page 78
Stone figure at the Cathedral representing a Pilgrim .. ,, 92
The Norman House in the Courtyard of St. Mary's Guild-
hall .. .. ,, 96
Monks' Abbey .. .. ,, 103
A Stone Head on the Cathedral .. .. ,, 106
Wood carving in Cathedral of Fox preaching to Geese .. ,, 110
St. Mary's Conduit .. .. ,, 111
The House of the Grey Friars .. .. ,, 112
The Seal of the Malandry .. .. ,, 116
St. Giles' Hospital .. .. ,, 118
Statue in the Cathedral from the Hospital of St. Giles .. ,, 119
High Bridge Chapel .. .. ,, 132
Saxon Long and Short Work .. .. ,, 135
The Outer Exchequer Gate, known as " The Magazine
House" .. .. ,, 140
Interior of the Old Meeting House of the Lincoln Society
of Friends .. .. ,, 149
The Lower Room in the House of the Grey Friars .. ,, 157
The Close Gatehouse which stood at the western end of
Eastgate .. .. ,, 172
Boundary Stone between the Bail and the City .. .. ,, 180
East Gate of the Close which stood near the Deanery .. ,, 181
The Old Registry (North side) .. .. ,, 183
Dunston Pillar .. .. ,, 194
A Poster advertising a Witham Steamer .. .. .. ,, 197
A Lincoln Tram .. .. ,, 209
Pottergate Arch (North side) .. .. ,, 226
The Old Registry, or North Gate of the Close, which
occupied the site of Priory Gate .. .. .. ,, 228

Maps

Picture Map .. .. End Paper
Roman Lincolnshire .. .. Page 13
Roman Lincoln .. .. ,, 18
Churches in 1066 .. .. ,, 31
Open Fields and Turnpike Roads .. .. ,, 191
Map of City .. .. End Paper

FOREWORD.

For three thousand years men have been living on the hill where Lincoln stands today. During all that time they have been engaged in the great task of organising their common life, in the form of a rude Celtic village, a Roman city, or a self-governing municipality. They are still engaged on it, more busily perhaps, certainly more consciously, than ever before, since, for the first time in Lincoln's long history, every adult person, man or woman, has a right to a voice in its common affairs. How they have set about this task of living together from earliest time to the present day makes up the story of Lincoln as it is told in this book, and the authors will be disappointed if, in the telling, they have not quickened the interest of the reader in the community in which he lives, and made him more willing to take an active part in its affairs. The education of the modern citizen, we have recently been told, "should make him feel himself to be consciously at one with the community, sharing in its traditions of the past, its life and action in the present, its aspirations and responsibilities in the future." Perhaps it is the special function of local history study to stimulate this consciousness ; at least, it is difficult to find a subject which so closely relates to the problems which the modern citizen has to face. The group life of the city epitomises the wider life of the nation, and its problems are, in the main, different in degree rather than in kind. If the study of local history can contribute to the quality of citizenship in the democratic community of today, it need make no apology for claiming a place in the reading of children at school, or for that matter, of their parents at home, and when once the art of presenting it has been discovered, we believe that local history can make this contribution. Our hope in writing this book is, that where we have failed others will succeed in finding out how it can best be utilised to this important end.

A word may be said on the division of labour between the two authors. One has had the task of collecting the material, the other of presenting it. Both are conscious of shortcomings in the way they have performed their respective tasks, but to compress the long and varied story of Lincoln into 225 pages was not easy.

The authors are indebted to Mr. J. W. F. Hill, not only for much unpublished material, but also for very helpful suggestions and criticism. They also wish to acknowledge the help which they have received from the members of the Lincoln Education Committee and from Mr. C. W. Hooton, without whose initiative and constant encouragement, the book would not have been written.

Thanks are also due to Mr. F. T. Baker and Mr. L. F. Fuller for their criticism and help in reading the proofs ; to Mrs. S. Smith for allowing photographs by the late Mr. S. Smith to be used for preparing several of the line drawings ; to the Dean and Chapter of the Cathedral for permission to use drawings in their possession for making other of the line drawings ; to the Usher Gallery Committee for permission to reproduce pictures and drawings in their collection, and to the Director of the Library and Art Gallery (Mr. F. J. Cooper) for his assistance ; to the City Council and the Town Clerk (Mr. G. H. Banwell) for the loan of blocks for some of the illustrations ; and to Mr. Austin Garland for his helpful advice on the production of the book.   E.I.A.
                                                                J.D.C.

Second Edition.   *December,* 1947.

" The Story of Lincoln" has been revised and brought up to date by the addition of a short account of Lincoln during the war of 1939-45. The authors wish to make their grateful acknowledgments to Miss K. Major and others for their helpful criticisms and suggestions.   E.I.A.
                                                                J.D.C.

CHAPTER I

LOOKING BACKWARD.

Lincoln is a very old town, one of the oldest in England. Suppose for a minute we stand still and imagine ourselves flying back through the ages—a hundred years, five hundred years, a thousand years, and still more—to the times when Lincoln began. What changes should we see ? Before we had flown back a hundred years we should notice the city getting smaller ; the factories, for instance, would be gone, as also would a large number of houses in the industrial parts of the town. The straggling suburbs also would disappear and in their places would be meadows and corn-fields, and in a very short time, say by 1830, the railways would vanish and instead of the busy city of 70,000 people which Lincoln is today, we should have a quiet country town, white with apple-blossom in spring—it was known as "the city of orchards"—with coaches, country carts, flocks of sheep, pedlars and packhorses wending their way along the muddy roads to market.

But we are far, very far, from the beginning of Lincoln. To get there we must fly in great leaps of two hundred or three hundred years at a time. But what a succession of great and exciting events we shall see ; the Civil War, for instance, and the coming of the Roundheads in 1644 to drive out the Cavaliers. There is fighting in the streets and scenes of violence in the cathedral. Then as the years glide by, we see the Lincolnshire Rising in 1536, when 2,500 rebels gathered in Lincoln to protest against the work of Henry VIII and his ministers. Kings and queens come in state to visit the city, and medieval parliaments are assembled here.

Population 75,000.

And as we go back through the centuries to the Middle Ages we notice the town becoming not less, but more lively ; its streets thronged with merchants (many of them from the German cities of the Baltic) and with Jews ; boats are coming up the Fossdyke and the Witham and strings of horses and mules laden with bales of wool are moving along the roads. Lincoln is obviously an important town ; in fact it is a staple town. Edward I has just ordained that no wool can be sent out of Lincolnshire except through Lincoln, and whether they like it or not, the wool merchants have to bring it there to sell, and go there to buy. That is why it is called a staple town. And a fine town it is, with the cathedral only a century old, still dazzling white in the sunshine on the crest of Lincoln hill ; and side by side with it, the castle with its high thick walls, sally ports and great shell keep. Like the cathedral, it is built of limestone from the neighbouring quarry, and after the repairs of Edward's reign, it stands spick and span, ready to face a siege if the turmoil of the Barons' wars breaks out again.

Lincoln has already seen two periods of civil war ; one in 1217, when the rebellious barons, who had called in the help of Prince Louis of France, were trapped in the steep streets of Lincoln at the famous Lincoln Fair ; and the other about three quarters of a century earlier, when Stephen and Matilda fought for the crown of England. At that time, Lincoln was one of the biggest and most important towns in the country, with many merchants and rich Jews, and both sides wished to possess it. Indeed, since the Normans ravaged Yorkshire and the northern counties, Lincoln has been the capital of the north. The Normans have built a strong castle here and forced the conquered Danes and English to pull down 166 houses to make room for it, for they cannot afford to let so rich a town as Lincoln with its many merchants, fall into the hands of the Saxon thegns and Danish jarls who are gathering in Yorkshire to drive them out. The Norman conquest is only the first we shall see as we travel backwards. Within two hundred years the Danes come streaming into the country along the Roman roads and up the rivers, burning and pillaging—finally settling down into good Lincolnshire yeomen. And three or four hundred years further back we see the Angles and Saxons pushing their way inland from the coast and the country people flying in terror to take refuge behind the massive walls of the Roman city of Lincoln. This great city has already been in existence nearly four hundred years, and is one of the finest in Roman Britain ; but though the Romans came so many years ago—before 50 A.D.—they are not the first people to live on the spot where Lincoln stands today. For five hundred years, seven hundred years—who knows ?—there has been a village of the Celts here, a mere cluster of rude huts, and even this may not be the first settlement on this ancient site. It is possible, but not certain, that the Celts found a still earlier people in possession—different from themselves and from us—darker, shorter, living in caves or holes in the ground, hunting the animals in the forests, digging pits for them with their stone tools and defending themselves with their stone weapons. But they are no match for the Celts with their bronze shields and bucklers, and are soon either driven away into the hills or enslaved.

We do not know for certain that these early men lived on the site of Lincoln, but we know that they passed this way, because things which they used have been found—a few stone axes called 'celts' and a small stone hammer. The date of these objects cannot definitely be fixed, but it is certainly not later than 1,000 B.C. and they may have been brought from other sites in the county where many similar objects have been found.

Suppose we leave Lincoln for a little while and circle round the neighbouring countryside. How different it is from today ! On

all sides are almost endless woods and marshes where now there are
fields or villages.   Here and there are clearings where men are
trying to cultivate the ground, but the most striking things of all
are the large mounds scattered about the country, especially along
the tops of the hills.   Some are the 'long barrows', or burial places,
of a still earlier people who have been wandering about the slopes
of Lincolnshire since the time of Abraham.   Here and there are
'round barrows' of more recent tribesmen.   One of these at
Riseholme, quite near to Lincoln, may be seen to this day.

THE TRACKWAY.

But if we have really been using our eyes, we shall have found
out something else.   We have often wondered why Lincoln sprang
up just where it did and not somewhere else, and as we look down
at the country around Lincoln, especially to the north and south,
we can see the reason.   Along the tops of the hills is something
that looks like a long white ribbon running all the way from the
Humber to the big hill where Lincoln stands.   The ribbon runs
down the side of the hill and is then stopped by the marshes and
stagnant pools left by the sluggish Witham.   It is taken up again
on the other side and goes on for miles, right into the heart of the
downland country of Norfolk, where the men of the stone age
found their best flints, and where the flint pits they dug may be seen
to this day.   It is the trackway which they made as they padded
stealthily along the tops of the limestone hills in search of food,
shelter and pasture for their animals.   It had been used for at least
a thousand years when the Romans came, and it is the key to the
history of Lincoln.

THE SITE OF LINCOLN.

At the point where the trackway crossed the gap in the hills
made by the Witham two streams of travellers crossed, one using

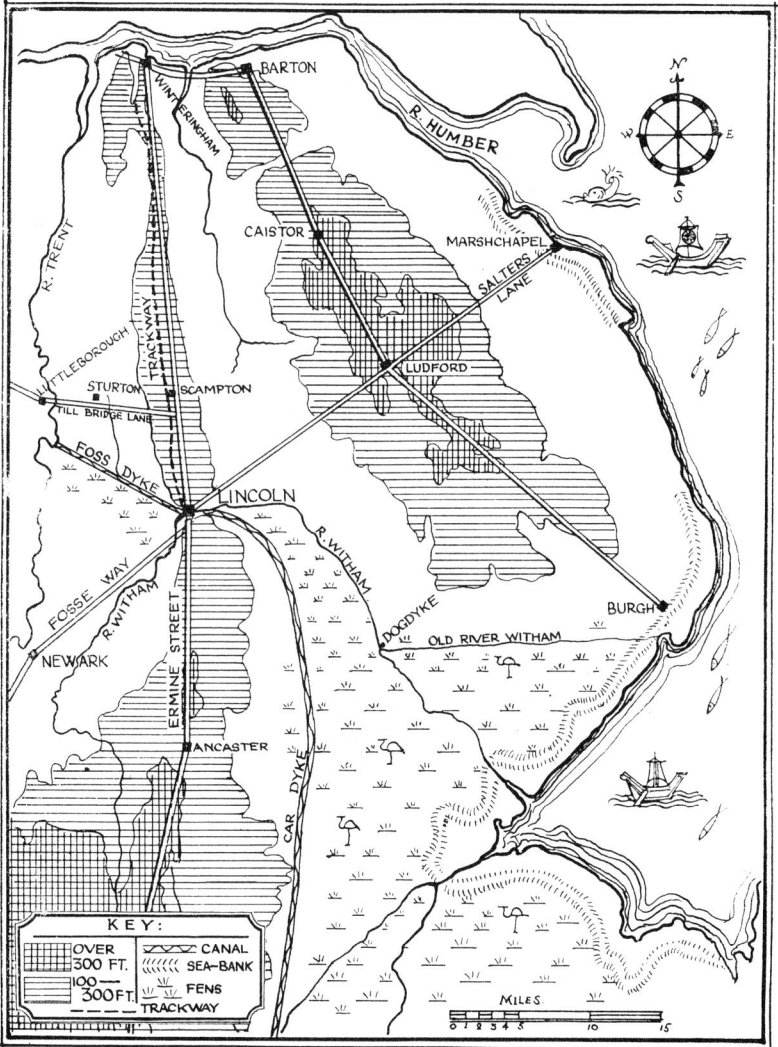

Roman Lincolnshire

boats along the river, the other passing along the trackway.   Here
was a good site for a trading settlement, and it was to become a
centre for the Roman road system and the modern railways.

We have now travelled back three thousand years, and during
all that time there have been men in and around Lincoln, struggling
to build up a community in which they could enjoy the two great
boons of peace and freedom.   That is why they came to Lincoln.
They were safer here than anywhere else because from Lincoln hill
they could watch the approach of strangers from the north, and they
were protected on the south and west by marshes and the shallow
pools left by the Witham.   No wonder the Celtic tribesmen who
came from Germany had a village here, and what is more natural
than that the Romans, when they pushed their way up the old pre-
historic track and came to the hill of Lincoln, decided that here
was a spot designed by nature for a permanent camp?   They
swept away the humble Celtic settlement but they kept its name.
The Celts probably called it Lindon, a word which contains the
same word as the Welsh " Llyn," meaning a lake.   Then as the
city grew the Romans latinized this early name and added the
word Colonia, and so it became Lindum Colonia, the name of
one of the finest cities in Roman Britain.

CHAPTER II.

ROMAN LINCOLN.

So far we have been in the twilight of pre-history, with nothing but a handful of flints and an old trackway to guide us. But between 43 A.D. and 50 A.D. the Romans overran the south and west, and then swept along the line of the old trackway towards the north. At a single bound Lincoln came into recorded history. The Romans arrived at the Celtic village of Lindon about 45 A.D. and destroyed it. Not a single trace of it remains today. They set up a camp on the crest of the hill and established a garrison of legionaries. It consisted of the 9th Legion, a body of about 6,000 men, probably Spaniards, who were

Tombstone of a Standard Bearer of the 9th Legion

not merely soldiers but also engineers, builders, navvies, farmers ; in fact, anything and everything, as need arose.

Gradually, as the fierce tribesmen of Yorkshire and the north were conquered, Lincoln ceased to be a frontier fortress and became a great city, one of the finest in Britain, a centre of trade and the seat of Government for a large area around. Perhaps the best way of looking at Roman Lincoln would be to try to see it through the

The Romans arrived c.47/48 A.D. The timber defences of the legionary fortress have now been located by excavation and found to coincide with the line of the later Roman wall and to enclose 42 acres. They had timber gates and timber interval towers inserted later.

eyes of the retired Roman soldiers who lived there. Lincoln was the home of many retired soldiers, for it was the custom to allow veterans who were too old for active service to settle down on a farm near one of the towns, so that they would form a trained reserve in case of attack. Such towns were frequently called colonies, and the word Lincoln is derived from Lindum Colonia, since Lincoln was a "colony" of retired soldiers. Now we know something of one of these soldiers be-

Tombstone of Gaius Julius Galenus

cause his tombstone was dug up in 1859, and it tells us a great deal about him. His name was Gaius Julius Galenus. He came from Lyons in Gaul, and belonged to the sixth legion. He had been stationed at York and had no doubt taken part in many fights which the sixth legion had had with

the tribes of the north. At length he was discharged and sent to Lincoln, where (let us imagine) he was given a piece of land and told that he might settle down in peace for the rest of his days. Let us follow Gaius on his way from York, which was then called Eboracum, to Lindum. There would be many parties of soldiers, merchants, and officials, travelling between the two cities along the fine roads which the Romans had built, and Gaius would probably travel with one of these.

THE APPROACH TO LINCOLN.

To reach Lindum the party would have to cross the Trent. There was no bridge, but at Segelocum—Littleborough it is now—

Usher Gallery)

NEWPORT ARCH

(As it appeared in 1780)

(Collection

the Romans had built a stone causeway across the river, by which it was possible to cross, but at the expense of getting wet ; you can still see a part of it today when the water is very low.   Having crossed safely—no easy matter if the river was full—Gaius would travel straight along the road which we now call Till Bridge Lane, until he reached Ermine Street, about three miles north of Lindum. We do not know exactly at what period Gaius came to Lindum, but let us suppose he came when Lindum was at the height of its prosperity, that is, about the year 330 A.D.   As he travelled along he would pass many well cultivated farms, with good houses or villas standing in spacious grounds.   The country was so peaceful that there was no need to live inside walled towns, and rich Britons and Romans often preferred to settle down in the open country.   He would pass at least two of these large country houses, at Sturton and Scampton, and would see the slaves at work in the fields, and would stop now and then to admire the fine plumage of the pheasants which the Romans introduced as pets to give colour to their gardens and grounds.

Ermine Street, which Gaius soon reached, is a long straight road, well paved and raised on a high bank in many places to ensure good drainage.   Long before he arrived at Lindum he would be able to see its white walls standing on the very top of Lindum hill, and as he drew nearer he would be able to distinguish tall buildings which rose above the walls—the basilica and the temple. The city was built of limestone from the neighbouring quarries, and though many of the buildings would be a hundred or two hundred years old when Gaius saw them, they would still be white and clean and untarnished by smoke, since the Romans used only wood in their house fires, and of course had no factory chimneys at all. What a fine sight the city must have made as Gaius came swinging along Ermine Street towards the great gatehouse now known as

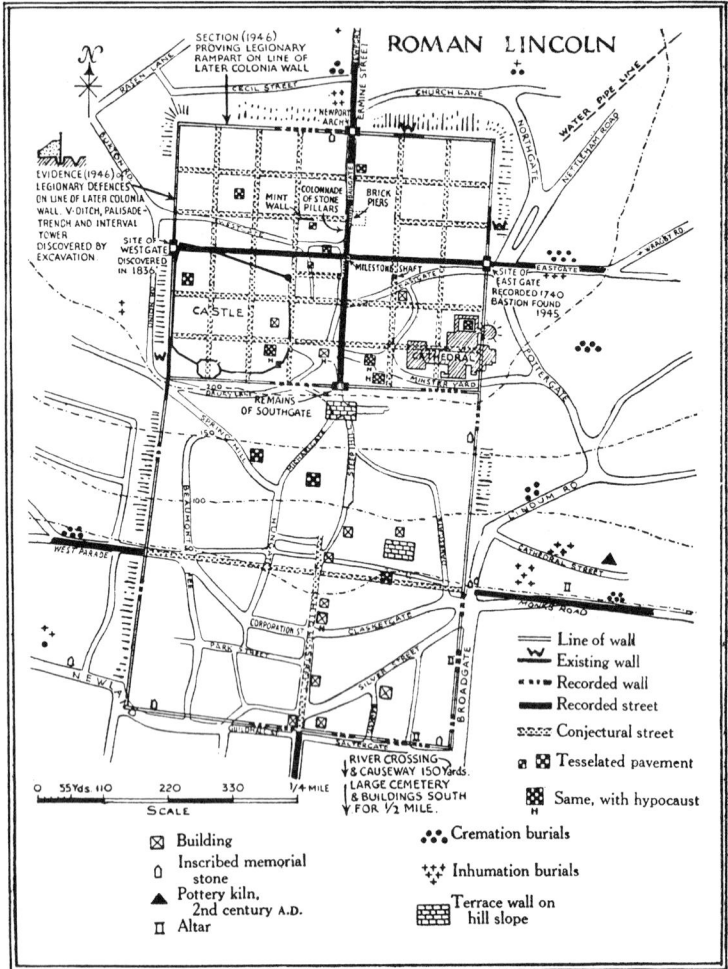

Map labels and legend:

ROMAN LINCOLN

SECTION (1946) PROVING LEGIONARY RAMPART ON LINE OF LATER COLONIA WALL

WATER PIPE LINE

CECIL STREET

CHURCH LANE

NEWPORT ARCH

EVIDENCE (1946) OF LEGIONARY DEFENCES ON LINE OF LATER COLONIA WALL. V-DITCH, PALISADE TRENCH AND INTERVAL TOWER DISCOVERED BY EXCAVATION

SITE OF WESTGATE DISCOVERED IN 1836

MINT WALL

COLONNADE OF STONE PILLARS

BRICK PIERS

MILESTONE SHAFT

SITE OF EASTGATE

SITE OF EAST GATE RECORDED 1740 BASTION FOUND 1945

CASTLE

CATHEDRAL

LAST REMAINS OF SOUTHGATE

WEST PARADE

CORPORATION ST.

RIVER CROSSING & CAUSEWAY 150 Yards.
LARGE CEMETERY & BUILDINGS SOUTH FOR ½ MILE.

0 55Yds. 110   220   330   1/4 MILE
SCALE

⊠	Building
◊	Inscribed memorial stone
▲	Pottery kiln, 2nd century A.D.
Π	Altar

Line of wall
Existing wall
Recorded wall
Recorded street
Conjectural street
Tesselated pavement
Same, with hypocaust
Cremation burials
Inhumation burials
Terrace wall on hill slope

Newport Arch, wondering what sort of a town he had been sent to settle in !

LINDUM FROM THE NORTH.

As he approached this massive gateway he would see stretching on either side of him the great north wall with its round towers at each end to protect the corners of the city, and, in front, a deep dry moat, a part of which can still be seen between Church Lane and East Bight. The wall was eighteen feet high, and consisted of a core of rubble held together by cement—you can still see a part of this near the moat—and faced with squared stones. In the middle of the wall was a massive gatehouse, something like the Stonebow of today. It had a large central archway, sixteen feet wide, and smaller gates called posterns on either side. The southern face of this gatehouse is now known as Newport Arch. Over the gateways was a guard room for the soldiers in charge of the gatehouse. The arch was originally twenty-two feet high, but the level of Lincoln has slowly risen until the old road is buried eight feet under the present roadway.

LINDUM FROM THE INSIDE.

Having passed the guard at the gatehouse, Gaius would be admitted inside the walls. Immediately in front of him he would find an open space, which ran all round the inside of the city walls, and was kept clear so that the soldiers could be moved rapidly to any part of the fortifications. Before him would be a broad main road, with side walks for foot passengers, which would take him to the heart of the city. Here he would find the Forum or market square. He would be able to buy anything he wanted after his long journey, and on the eastern side of the main street he would see the deep cistern which the Romans had constructed to supply the town with water. It was filled from a spring about a mile away

The gate was equipped with towers on the north side, rising above the height of the wall; one has been revealed by excavation.

just beyond the present boundary between Lincoln and Nettleham, and the water was brought in an earthenware pipe, which ran under a raised embankment on the east side of Ermine Street. The pipe was laid in a concrete bed to prevent it from bursting under the pressure necessary to drive the water up the hill to Lincoln. There is no trace of it today, but the cistern which it fed—known as the Blind Well—was not filled in until the middle of the eighteenth century. Here Gaius would no doubt find crowds of household slaves filling their earthenware pitchers with water and taking home provisions from the market for their masters' tables.

As Gaius walked along, he would see on his right two very fine groups of buildings, each having a row of high pillars in front of it. We have still much to

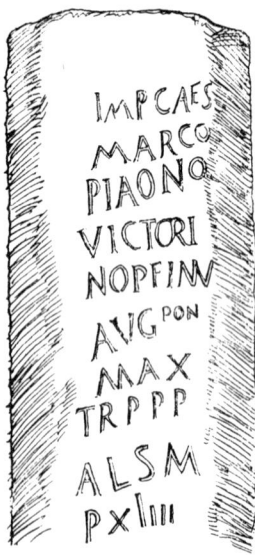

learn about Roman Lincoln but the first group probably contained the Forum and Basilica, or Town Hall—a very imposing building, one of the biggest ever built by the Romans in England. Here were the law courts, and the rooms occupied by the city governor and his officials. They were responsible not only for Lincoln itself, but for the district around, and it would be here that Gaius would report himself, and enquire for the land which, as a retired soldier, he was allowed to occupy. The Mint Wall is probably part of the north wall of the Basilica, and the bases of five of the pillars which stood in front of it can be found in three cellars under 25, 26 and 27 Bailgate. The positions

Roman Milestone found in Bailgate

The "Blind Well" was *not* the reservoir; foundations for a storage tank have been located by excavation behind the north wall from the interval tower in East Bight for some distance east and possibly to the next interval tower still to be located.

of other pillar bases are marked by rings of setts in the road.

The second building Gaius would see was probably a temple into which he may have gone to offer thanks for his safe journey—and between the temple and the Basilica lay the main road running east and west. At the point where it crossed the north to south road stood a tall milestone which showed the distance between Lindum and Segelocum, and would, no doubt, remind Gaius of how he had waded across the Trent. It gave the distance to Segelocum as fourteen Roman miles. This stone is now in the city museum and you may see the distance marked on it for yourself. Perhaps we may leave Gaius here, thankful that he has finished his travels and that he has been lucky enough to be sent to so fine a town as Lindum to end his days in peace.

THE PLAN OF THE CITY.

We can now explore the city a little further for ourselves. It has not been allowed to grow anyhow, like modern cities, but was laid out in rectangular blocks by streets running parallel to the four main roads. The side streets were narrow, but the four main roads were broad and smooth, with side walks for pedestrians, and an underground sewer to carry away the drainage. In some places the ròads were constructed of a thick layer of concrete laid on a foundation of rubble ; in others they consisted of six layers of stones, one on top of the other, the largest at the bottom, and were finished off with a surface of gravel or, sometimes, of hot lime in order to make the road as waterproof as possible.

Many of the houses on the main roads were very big and fine, with tesselated pavements and hypocausts—which is the Roman word for central heating. There is, at this present time, a very good example of a hypocaust under the Precentory.

The Precentory is *now* the Deanery.

In the side streets, the houses were smaller and, perhaps, built of wood, since it was here that the poorer people lived. At first the whole area was roughly some thirty-eight acres ; 440 yards long on the eastern and western sides, and 425 on the north and south sides. It was surrounded by walls pierced by gates. The one on the north we have already seen. On the east was the East Gate, near which was a concrete platform placed just inside the city, upon which a large catapult would probably stand. Through the gate ran the road leading to the salt pans near Marsh Chapel, which was afterwards known as Salters' Lane. The western gate was smaller and had no main road running from it since it overlooked the sparsely populated and marshy lowlands of the Trent valley. This gate was completely buried when the Normans threw up the earthworks of the Castle, and it was not uncovered until 1836, but no trace of it remains visible today. Along the crest of the hill which overlooks the Witham ran the south wall, and in the middle was the South Gate, of which traces can still be seen in the wall of No. 26 Steep Hill.

But this enclosure at the top of the hill soon became too small, and the Romans had to extend it by continuing the eastern and western walls to the edge of the marsh in the Witham valley. The new east wall with its moat ran across land which now forms the grounds of the Usher Gallery. It then ran along the west side of Broadgate to a spot near Thornbridge. The west wall ran down Motherby Hill and the Park as far as Newland, and the two ends were joined together by a south wall in the middle of which was a gatehouse, on the site of which the Stonebow now stands.

If you walked straight down the hill and through the old South Gate towards the new South Gate, you would pass through a busy street lined with substantial buildings, of which an interesting relic may still be seen in the cellar of the shop now occupied by Messrs.

The north tower of the East Gate was found by excavation in 1964 and is displayed in the forecourt of Eastgate Hotel: a matching tower was located in the Tennyson Green opposite.

A 4th century gate in the extended west wall was uncovered by excavation in 1970/1; it lies between Orchard Street and The Park.

Boots at the corner of Clasketgate, and as you proceeded through the new South Gate, you would come almost immediately upon the wharves where the ships which brought merchandise to the city were moored—silk and wine and olive oil from Gaul and Italy—and took away cargoes of wheat to Rome and other cities.

ENGINEERING WORKS.

You might wonder how these ships could reach Lincoln, so far away from the sea. But the Romans were exceedingly clever engineers and they had improved the existing waterways so much that Lindum could be reached by water from two sides. They had dug the Fossdyke so that boats should be able to pass from the Witham at Lindum to the Trent at Torksey ; they had also straightened and deepened the Witham between Lindum and Chapel Hill, so that it was possible for boats to reach Lindum from the sea. And above all they had dug the great channel known now as the Cardyke, one of the greatest engineering feats in England prior to modern times. It was fifty miles long and stretched from Washingborough to the Nene at Peterborough and was in some places fifty feet wide. But the Romans did not go to all this trouble merely to make Lindum an inland port ; they had another and more powerful reason. They wished to protect the city and the country round about it from floods. At the time the Romans came, two great swamps lay to the south-east and south-west, separated by a narrow neck of dry land. The Romans built a raised causeway over this, and in order to prevent it from being flooded by storm water from the upper Witham, they cut the Sincil Dyke to carry the flood water across the loop formed by the natural course of the river. The dyke joined the river again at a point near Stamp End, well below the city roads and wharves. But their greatest danger came from the Trent. At one time the Trent and Witham had formed one river, and although they were now separate, the watershed

The remains under Messrs. Boots is of the hypocaust of a public bath building. A public fountain was found on the east side of High Street under Messrs. Meakers shop in 1953.

between them was very low. When the Trent rose to flood heights, the water would pour through the four gaps in the hills—at Spalford, Newton, Torksey and Brampton—and submerge the surrounding country. How did the Romans meet this difficulty? They built banks across the four gaps, and by this means the waters of the Trent were kept back for more than a thousand years. But in 1795, when the Spalford bank burst, twenty thousand acres to the west of Lincoln were flooded to a depth of ten feet, and the people of Saxilby had to take refuge in the church! The Romans also dug the Cardyke, as we have seen, to catch the water from the highlands south of Lincoln and to save the fens from floods.

THE CITY FROM THE SOUTH.

Roman Milestone found at the western end of Sibthorp Street

Now suppose we follow the road through the South Gate out towards Leicester and London. Within fifty yards or so we notice the road sloping down to the ford where the High Bridge stands today. (This is the second ford we have met, but no bridge. Evidently the Romans did not mind getting wet on their journeys; it shows also that there must have been very little wheeled traffic on the roads). Then we pass along the raised causeway, and before long come to the first milestone on the road to Leicester. It was set up about the year 260 and may be seen to this day in two parts, one in High Street near the wall between the shops numbered 110 and 111, and the other—the part which bears the inscription—in the Museum.

Evidence of a Roman timber bridge was found in 1950 when the river was drained to allow for repairs to the High Bridge and alteration to the bed of the river.

The stone in High Street is not the same geological material as the milestone in the Museum: therefore the two cannot be related.

We are now some dis-
tance to the south of Roman
Lincoln, and as we look back
at the city behind us, we
realise the great skill and
determination of the Ro-
mans. There it lies, a great
rectangle of stone, stretching
down the side of the hill
almost to the banks of the
Witham, with its broad main
streets cutting it into smaller
rectangles; its Forum, Basilica and Temples, all of
white limestone, making an
ordered cluster on the very
brow of the hill, and its main
street backed with fine
houses and shops. And

Part of a Roman Milestone
110 High Street

around it all is the high stone wall pierced by its massive gates..
Surely the Romans were to stay for ever !

The road we are standing on, the famous Ermine Street, which
runs direct to London, consists of a thick layer of concrete laid
on a bed of gravel and earth, resting on piles driven into the
marshes. A few yards further on it is joined by a still more famous
road, the Fosse Way to Newark, Leicester, and on to Exeter. This
is another of those ribbons of stone which the Romans made to
bind their great empire together.

Thus Lincoln was drawn into the great net which the Romans,
by means of their wonderful roads, flung over Western Europe.

From Scotland to Palestine, from the Danube to the Nile, the
Romans had established their sway, and the many different peoples
of this vast area were made to submit to the rules of conduct which
their Roman masters laid down.   The upper classes among the
natives learned Latin ; they became Roman citizens, and took part
in the government of their own cities and of the Empire, and
whatever their nationality, they obeyed one law.   Shall we ever see
again such unity among the peoples of Western Europe ? But we
must never forget, it was based on slavery, and that, perhaps is one
reason why it could not endure.   We can imagine, for instance, how
the native tribesmen must have toiled to build and keep in repair
the roads and drainage works round Lincoln, and how they must
have cursed the day that brought them under the Roman yoke.

THE END OF ROMAN LINCOLN.

Lindum was a part of this great unity, one of hundreds of cities
which made up the Roman Empire.   But the splendid roads and
waterways which linked them together helped also to destroy them.
Lindum was easily approached both by land and water, and as
early as 287 A.D. there was a raid on the Lincolnshire coast by
Saxon pirates.   The walls were probably rebuilt or strengthened
about that time and the city continued to enjoy a period of prosperity
and peace lasting up to 340 A.D.   Then the raids of the Saxons
recommenced.   There was also civil war among the Roman-Britons
and invasions of the Picts and Scots.   Probably the richer citizens
deserted the town before 400 A.D.   The Roman legions were called
away to other parts of the front and the barbarians from Ireland,
Scotland and Germany poured in.   There was a long period of
fierce fighting and during its course Lindum was taken by the Angles
and burnt (as we can tell from the blackened ruins of the Basilica).
For a time the city may have been an almost deserted ruin.   The
Roman period was over and the Dark Ages had begun.

CHAPTER III.

SAXON AND DANISH LINCOLN.

If you look at the map you will see how easy it would be for the barbarians to reach Lincoln. Three roads—from the north, east and south—and two waterways, the Witham and the Fossdyke from the Trent, converge on it, and we can imagine what longing eyes the Angles and Saxons, and also, perhaps, the Picts and Scots, cast on this rich and beautiful city. What exactly happened we do not know. There was terror and confusion for many years. We hear the names of Vortigern, the British King, and Hengist, the war leader of the Jutes. We even hear of King Arthur, who is supposed to have reconquered Lincoln from the invaders about 490, and also Hengist's daughter, Rowena, who is said to have married Vortimer, the son of Vortigern, and poisoned him in order to get his kingdom. He is reported to have been buried in Lincoln, but no one knows where.

The struggle was long and bitter. It lasted for a hundred and fifty years, the German invaders always pressing the Romanised Celts further westward and northward into the hills and barren uplands, while the rich lowlands were occupied by horde after horde of Angles and Saxons. Look down the road leading north and south of Lincoln and notice the number of places ending in 'ham' and 'ton' and you will see where they settled. Not one Celtic name survives in all the stretch of road from north to south except the 'Llyn' in Lincoln ! And if you search the whole of Lincolnshire, you will find very few. And how many Celtic words have survived ? Half-a-dozen, or perhaps, a dozen—bin (*e.g.*, cornbin), dun (*e.g.*, dun colour), coombe (small valley) and one or two more are the only ones that were taken over from the native Celts. It looks almost as if the Celtic people of Lincolnshire and the other lowland counties of England were wiped out. Hardly a trace of them remains either in our language or our place names. We do not find this complete disappearance of the old speech anywhere else in the whole Roman Empire. Are we to conclude that our Germanic ancestors were more ruthless in their treatment of the conquered people than the Goths or the Vandals or the Franks who conquered other parts of the Roman Empire ?

LINCOLN UNDER THE ANGLES.

Lincoln itself was seized by a band of Anglian invaders who became known as the Lindiswaras. Another war band, known as the Gainas, occupied North Lincolnshire ; and these two bands, with others, combined to form the kingdom of Mercia, which came into being about 584. During this period of confusion, Lincoln itself was probably deserted, but after the formation of the kingdom of Mercia towards the end of the sixth century it was re-occupied, and as the country became settled the city slowly came to life again. It also became Christian again.

In 630, Edwin, the Christian King of Northumbria, became supreme over the North of England, and Lindsey passed under his protection. Paulinus, the great missionary who had converted Edwin, visited Lincoln and is said to have converted the local reeve, Blecca, and his family, and a church was built. Perhaps it was on the site of the cathedral or the present church of St. Paul, but no one knows for certain. Another church, St. Martin's at Dernstall, was probably built at this time, too. We may conclude from this that the ruined city was at last stirring into a new life under its new masters. But we can form little idea of what Anglian Lincoln

The church of St. Paul-in-the-Bail was declared redundant in 1967 and is to be demolished in 1971.

was like. The Germanic invaders were farmers and countrymen and they hated towns ; they were anxious to find good corn growing and pasture land on which to settle, and were loth to sleep within the shadow of the Roman cities which they had looted and burned. But we can see from the names of the early churches of Lincoln that the invaders in course of time settled both inside and outside the Roman city.

If you turn to the map on page 31 you will see St. Paul's Church in the middle of the upper city, and St. Martin's in the middle of the lower city, besides several others, St. Swiwithin's St. Edmund's, St. Cuthbert's and St. Lawrence's.

Old St. Martin's Church
Partly demolished 1871.   Tower in 1921

But you will notice three churches outside the walls—St. Peter's St. Austin's and St. Rumbold's, which shows that some of the English settlers, at any rate, preferred to live outside the walls.

THE DANES.

The progress which Lincoln was making under the English was checked for a time by the coming of the Danes.   They came first in 839 and plundered the whole district with great slaughter.   They came again in 869, and in 873 they actually spent the whole winter at Torksey, and by 876 they had established themselves in Lincoln itself. It became one of their most important cities and together with Nottingham, Derby, Leicester and Stamford, formed the confederacy of the Five Burghs, or strongholds, which managed the affairs of this part of Danish England. But strong as the Five Burghs were, they fell to the attack of Edward the Elder, the son of Alfred the Great, and Aethelred, the famous ealdorman of Mercia. As these leaders advanced against the Danes, they erected lines of 'burghs' or fortresses with moats and palisades, from which raids were made on the towns and villages in which the Danes settled. The Danes were now farmers and merchants, with wives and families and possessions to lose, and rather than see them destroyed by the advancing English they gave way and yielded up

Danish Comb Case found at Lincoln

their strong places. By 918 the Five Burghs were surrendered, and the territories around them were cut up into shires like those of Wessex and the southern counties. Except for a rising in 942 there was peace in England until nearly the end of the century. Then came another avalanche of Danish invaders. Again and again the villages of Lindsey were ravaged. The monasteries were ruined by crushing fines ; the churches stripped of everything of value. At last, in 1013, Swegn, King of Denmark, who had established a camp at Gainsborough, obtained the surrender of Lincoln itself, and after a brief struggle with Ethelred the Redeless and Edmund Ironside, his son Canute became king in 1016. Except for a short period of civil war on his death in 1035, Lincolnshire enjoyed a period of peace until that amazing year 1066, when the whole history of England was changed by the results of a single battle. During this fifty years of peace, Lincoln grew and prospered, and became once more one of the leading centres of the country.

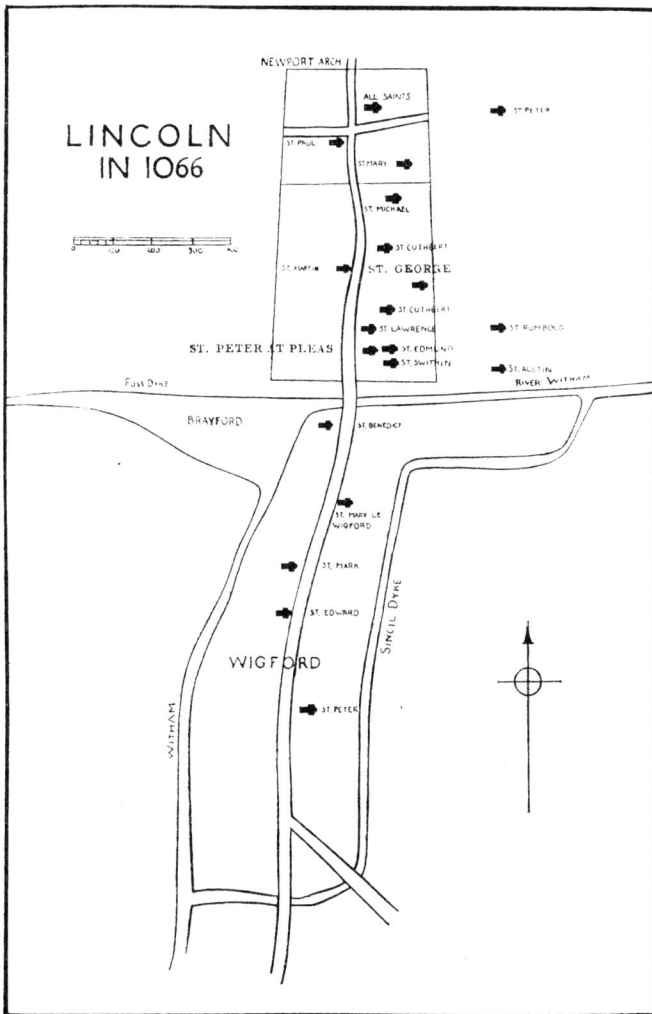

LINCOLN IN 1066

NEWPORT ARCH

ALL SAINTS

ST. PETER

ST. PAUL

ST. MARY

ST. MICHAEL

ST. CUTHBERT

ST. MARTIN

ST. GEORGE

ST. CUTHBERT

ST. LAWRENCE

ST. RUMBOLD

ST. PETER AT PLEAS

ST. EDMUND

ST. SWITHIN

ST. AUSTIN

FOSS DYKE

RIVER WITHAM

BRAYFORD

ST. BENEDICT

ST. MARY LE WIGFORD

ST. MARK

ST. EDWARD

SINCIL DYKE

WIGFORD

WITHAM

ST. PETER

Churches in 1066

DANISH LINCOLN.

In some ways the Danish period of Lincoln history is one of the greatest of all. Never before, not even under the Romans, and never since, has it taken so important a place among the great cities of the country. That may be rather surprising, but a moment's thought will show the reason. Consider the position of Lincoln, with its network of roads to all parts of the country,

Great Bargate
Demolished c. 1756

and the two rivers, the Witham and the Trent (via the Fossdyke), which connect it with the sea. Remember also, that the Danes were the greatest merchants and finest business men north of the Mediterranean, with trading connections from Stockholm to Constantinople, both by sea and land. The furs, hides, whale oil, walrus tusks and coarse woollen cloth in which the Danes traded could easily be brought to Lincoln and exchanged for the honey, malt and slaves of England. Owing to this vigorous trade with Scandinavia, a new suburb began to develop along the High Street between the Witham and Sincil Dyke, and by the end of the tenth century it had reached the site of the Bargates. This was Wigford (derived from the Norse word, VIK, meaning a creek or river), and was a separate community outside the boundary of the city itself, with its own common, the

LITTLE BARGATE
(From a painting by Peter de Wint, 1784-1849)

South Common, which kept its rights distinct from the other commons of the town until modern times.

With the growth of Wigford, the Roman south wall and ditch would no longer be necessary, and the ditch was gradually filled in to form the line of streets represented by Saltergate and Guildhall Street. Its place was eventually taken by the Sincil Dyke which defended the city on the south and east.

In time a wall was built along the bank of the Sincil Dyke to defend the approach to the city from the south. In this wall were two gatehouses, the Great Bargate defending the High Street, and Little Bargate, at the south-eastern corner of the suburb, defending the road to Canwick.

The western wall of the city was eventually continued south-ward to meet Brayford, on the banks of which stood a tower, afterwards known as the Lucy Tower. The road to the west passed out of the city by Newland Gate.

How many inhabitants were there in Lincoln before the Norman Conquest ? To answer this question we must go to the great record, Domesday Book, compiled by William the Conqueror in 1086. Here we learn that Lincoln, in the reign of Edward the Confessor, had 970 inhabited houses. Since the Danes reckoned six score

Newland Gate which stood near Lucy Tower Street

to the hundred—the 'long hundred' which is still used in marketing eggs in Lincolnshire—this comes to 1150, which, at the rate of five persons per house, represents a population of between five and six thousand. This was a large number for those days, and in fact, Lincoln probably never grew beyond it for the next six hundred years, until the great changes at the end of the eighteenth century caused the population to grow rapidly. It had also no fewer than eighteen churches, as you will see from the sketch map given on page 31.

Interesting relics of the Danish days of Lincoln are the silver pennies which were struck by the moneyers of Lincoln, who worked in small smithies in the town with their punches and dies. More than a thousand of their coins have been collected and may still be seen in the museum at Stockholm. They found their way to Scandinavia as Danegeld and in trade. Finally, the names of some of the streets recall the time when Lincoln was under Danish rule—Danesgate, Thorngate, Clasketgate, and at least ten others. 'Gate' is the Danish word for 'road'.

It should not be thought that all Lincoln street names ending in 'gate' date from before the Norman Conquest. Long after that time the people of this district still used Danish words. There was no 'Bail' in Lincoln before the Castle was built, and the name 'Bailgate' must, therefore, date from a period after the construction of the Castle.

Lincoln, during the Danish period, was not only a prosperous and growing town. It was also remarkably free. It was governed by twelve hereditary 'lawmen,' whose duty it was to interpret the laws and customs, and to act as judges over the people, with little interference by king, earl, or sheriff. The city paid Danegeld, and the citizens were liable for military service, but the people of the town, both Danish and English, were able to manage their local affairs through the hereditary lawmen in their own way. A great change, however, was on the way, and the freedom and prosperity of Lincoln was soon to receive a cruel blow.

CHAPTER IV.

NORMAN LINCOLN.

In 1068 William the Conqueror advanced into Northern England, and as he went he selected important points such as Nottingham, York, and Lincoln, at which to set up castles. He was afraid the conquered English and Danes might rise and overwhelm the handful of Norman knights, who, by the single battle of Hastings, had made themselves masters of England. The days of Lincolnshire's freedom were over. A king now ruled the counties who demanded taxes in money and services in kind, and required obedience to his will, and, in order to secure it, he cleared the top of Lincoln Hill and set up a castle there. A hundred and sixty-six houses had formerly stood here, but they had to go, together with their inhabitants, in order to make room for the Conqueror's castle. The unfortunate house-holders may even have been forced to pull down their own homes and pile up the embankments on which the castle walls stand, for the Norman garrison would certainly not do this manual labour themselves.

But besides the building of the castle, another and far more important event happened in Lincoln at this time. In order to strengthen the influence of the church, William encouraged the bishops to leave the small villages in which, until this time, many of them had preferred to live, and take up their residence in the large towns, and among the towns which were to have bishops was Lincoln.

The first bishop was Remigius, who was allowed to leave Dorchester, which had for many years been the seat of an enormous diocese, stretching from the Humber to the Thames, and build a cathedral at Lincoln. Like the builders of the castle, Remigius chose the highest possible ground for the site of his cathedral, and so the castle and the cathedral were erected almost side by side. The castle occupied the south western quarter of the upper Roman city and the cathedral began to rise in the south eastern. Again a considerable number of houses had to be cleared away, and their inhabitants with them. Possibly some of them obtained accommodation in the Butterwick district, where thirty-six houses were built on land specially granted by the king. It is thought that others settled in the new suburb of Newport, which began to grow up at this time. It had its own market and a church dedicated to St. Nicholas, the patron saint of merchants, and had most probably been formed by traders who brought their wares for sale to the gates of the old city, and set up a New Port or New Market there.

LINCOLN IN NORMAN TIMES.

Can we form a picture of Lincoln at this time ? William the Conqueror has left a detailed description in his famous Domesday Book. The king was anxious to know how much his new possessions were worth, and so he ordered an enquiry to be made from everybody who paid taxes to find out whether they were paying their fair share. The citizens of Lincoln were called on, in their turn, to come before the king's officers, and give details of all the property in the city ; how much each person had, how much it paid in taxes in Edward the Confessor's time, how much it paid at the time of the enquiry. Naturally, there were many disputes. In one case the citizens said the king had had certain taxes from thirty-three houses which the bishop held, while Ulviet the priest flatly denied this, and offered to prove his statement by the usual method of the ordeal of carrying hot iron. Bishop Remigius, Earl Hugh, the Abbot of Peterborough and many other important men, had not paid their taxes as they should, and some were accused of having seized the land belonging to others. The Domesday enquiry let daylight into many dark places !

It also showed that the city had suffered severely from the Conquest. Besides the 166 houses destroyed to make room for the castle, 74 others were said to 'lie waste' as a consequence of misfortune of fire, and 240 'mansions,' or blocks of dwelling houses which had existed in Edward the Confessor's time, had fallen into decay or been destroyed. What is the explanation of this terrible decline ? If we turn to a neighbouring town, Torksey, we see the same thing. Before the Conquest Torksey had 213 houses, more than Nottingham. Twenty years later half its houses were in ruins. Again, by the end of the century, the Fossdyke itself was silted up and practically impassable !

The people of Lincoln must have regarded the Norman Conquest as a calamity, and their new Norman masters as a curse. They pulled down houses to build a castle and a cathedral, as we have seen, and no doubt forced the inhabitants to supply labour and materials. They also made war on Lincoln's best customers, the Danes, because of the help they had given to the English during the Conquest, and so brought ruin to many Lincoln merchants. For a time the prosperity of Lincoln waned ; but Torksey was ruined and never recovered.

Lincoln remained a very important town, in spite of its sufferings. There were still many merchants there when the Domesday enquiry was made, and probably more than half its inhabitants lived by trade. The chief industry, of course, was agriculture, but Lincoln only had thirteen and a half carucates (about 1620 acres) of ploughed land, in addition to 231 acres in the hands of the king and the earl. This would not be sufficient to provide corn for so large a town, and no

doubt supplies had to come in (perhaps through Newport Market)
from the villages round about, in return for goods—cloth, weapons,
tools and pottery—which were made by Lincoln craftsmen.

But Lincoln was not only poorer, it was less free. It was no
longer the free self-governing burgh it had been under the Danes,
and the mild rule of Edward the Confessor. The twelve lawmen
still took their part, it is true, in the government of the city and
declared the laws and customs of the people in the Burgmanmot or
assembly of citizens ; but their power was not what it had been.
There was now a royal castle with its governor and garrison to
consider, also a bishop, and finally, the king's sheriff, who collected
the taxes for the king and could always call upon the castle for help
if his authority was challenged.   Lincoln had many years of struggle
before it achieved its independence again, and many calamities had
to be endured before it regained its prosperity.   In 1110, a terrible
fire consumed a great part of the town, the houses of which were
generally built of wood, and in 1124 the cathedral caught fire and
the roof was destroyed ; twice the town was shaken by earthquakes—
in 1142 and 1185—and more than all, there was the disaster of
civil war.

LINCOLN AND THE CIVIL WARS.

Why did Lincoln play so important a part in the miserable wars
of Stephen ?. Here we come again to the natural advantages of its
position. It commanded the routes from north to south, and
controlled one of the richest agricultural districts in all England.
The castle was so strong that only a small body of men was required
to hold it, and both sides did their best to get it, either by force or
fraud. First Matilda had it ; then Stephen. By means of a clever
ruse it was seized again by the supporters of Matilda. Stephen
returned and during 1141 laid vigorous siege to it. He stationed his

bowmen along the cathedral parapets, and placed catapults and slings on the West Front. An army was sent to its relief and a battle was fought on the hillside to the west of Lincoln. A large part of Stephen's army deserted. The rest was put to flight and the king was left alone surrounded by his enemies. He kept them off with his sword until it broke. He snatched up a battle axe from a Lincoln citizen, and stood at bay, "grinding his teeth and foaming like a mad boar," until someone knocked him down with a stone and forced him to surrender. In spite of all this excitement, the number of knights killed in the battle was very small. Medieval knights were perhaps kinder to one another in their battles than we might have expected. Possibly they valued a live prisoner, who would pay a ransom, much higher than a dead body that could only yield up its armour. But it was very different with the unfortunate citizens. They had favoured Stephen's cause and they had now to suffer the vengeance of Matilda's victorious army. The city was sacked, and the citizens put to the sword without mercy. Those who could, packed their goods on boats and took to the river until the fury was over.

Stephen made another attempt to take the castle, but he failed. In 1147 he had spent Christmas here, and was crowned in the cathedral, and in 1153 he made his peace with Matilda. From now onwards to the reign of Richard, Lincoln enjoyed a long period of peace. In 1194, however, the Constable of the Castle went over to the side of John, soon to be king, and the Chancellor, Longchamp, who ruled in Richard's absence, tried to capture the castle in the king's name. But he failed. For the third time in the century, Lincoln Castle withstood all the efforts of the besiegers, in spite of their catapults, mangonels, slings and rams. When Richard came home, the rebellious constable was deprived of his offices and lands, but he was restored by John.

Owing to the king's intolerable cruelties and oppressions the church, the barons and the merchants of the towns rose against him and forced him to grant the Great Charter at Runnymede. Only four of the original copies have survived and one of them— and the best of them—is at Lincoln. It had originally been sent by the barons to the Bishop of Lincoln, to be proclaimed by him in Bedford and Oxford, and was possibly given by Bishop Hugh of Wells at a later date to the dean and chapter of the cathedral. For centuries it was forgotten until it was discovered in 1810 by the Record Commissioners. It is now preserved in the cathedral as one of the greatest treasures in the city.

But another scene of violence was in store for Lincoln. John repudiated the Charter, collected an army of mercenaries and made war on the barons. In self defence they called in the aid of Prince Louis of France, and in 1216 seized the city of Lincoln, but were unable to get control of the castle. John died and his young son succeeded. He was innocent of his father's crimes, and many of the rebellious barons went over to him. William the Marshall, Earl of Pembroke, who ruled in the king's name, made it easy for them to desert the cause of the French prince. But Louis still remained in the country with a formidable army, and in 1217 his supporters again tried to seize Lincoln Castle. A desperate attempt was made to batter down the walls on the south and east sides, by the use of *perrières*—slings made to hurl specially heavy stones—but in vain. An army was collected at Newark

Figure on the Cathedral showing medieval costume

to relieve the sorely pressed garrison, and on May 19th, 1217, moved
out to Torksey on the way to Lincoln. William the Marshall, the
Commander in Chief of the royal army, decided to concentrate his
main attack on the West Gate of the city and Newport Arch, while
the garrison of the castle attempted a sally from the eastern gateway
into the city. The plan was a complete success. The Marshall's
men forced their way through the gates and over the walls, and the
besiegers found themselves caught between the attackers coming
through the Bail, and the party which had made a sally from the
castle. A confused fight in the narrow streets of Lincoln followed,
a hand to hand fight between mounted knights in which there was
no room to form ranks or charge, while footsoldiers slipped among
the combatants, stabbing and hamstringing the horses. The rebel
barons broke and fled, but were held up at the Great Bargate, which
could not be opened—some say, because a cow blocked the way.
Out of 611 knights and barons, four hundred with their servants
were taken prisoners, but the number reported killed was three.
The rest of the rebel army escaped. If, as the records tell us, only
three knights were killed in the Fair of Lincoln, as this battle is
sometimes called, it was not such a terrible business as we might
have expected, as least for the knights and men at arms. For the
citizens of Lincoln, however, it was very different. In accordance
with the custom of the time, the city was given up to plunder, and
the panic-stricken citizens adopted the measures which they had
found useful in the sack of 1141. They took to the river, loading
the boats with such valuables as they could carry. The city had
always been a centre of trade. It was wealthy and stocked with
merchandise which yielded a rich harvest to the plunderers. The
cathedral itself was not spared, since the canons of the cathedral
had been excommunicated for their opposition to John. It was used
as a barracks, and the fund collected for maintaining the fabric
stolen. " When they had thus seized on every kind of property,

so that nothing remained in any corner of the houses, they returned to their lords as rich men, and peace . . . having been declared throughout the city, they ate and drank amidst mirth and festivity."

Lincoln was never sacked again.   There was violence and disorder during the Civil War of the 17th century, but nothing like the brutal orgies of Stephen's time.   The city was growing richer every year, and where there is wealth there is power.   The citizens here, as in other growing towns, were attaining a position of respect and importance, and the king came to rely more and more upon them for support.   Above all, he looked to them for money ; he taxed them, their wool, hides and leather, which they exported ; the wine, cloth and luxuries which they imported.   And clearly, if they were to supply him with money, they must be protected by the law from violence and outrage.   Many of the barons, especially the smaller ones, and above all, the lawyers, clerks and officials who conducted the king's government, realised the necessity of peace and good administration.   Individual greed and brutality must not be allowed to defeat the common good, and even the king himself, be it the tyrant John, or the spendthrift Henry III, must be made to acknowledge the laws and customs of the land.   John was forced to accept Magna Carta.   Henry III was defeated in battle by Simon de Montfort.   Simon was killed and his party scattered ; but the king had learnt his lesson.   Edward I, who succeeded Henry III in 1272, carried on Simon's work, and made all classes, no matter how rich and powerful, serve the interests of the nation and acknowledge the law of the land.

We are now on the verge of Lincoln's period of greatness as a medieval city.   In spite of sacks and sieges, the city had been growing in prosperity.   It was becoming not merely a rich, but a beautiful city ; and more important still, it was one of the great centres of culture and civilisation in Western Europe. We can get some small idea of what it was like by looking at the buildings which have survived from that distant day. The cathedral, the Jews' House, the House of Aaron, St. Mary's Guildhall and the High Bridge, all contain Norman work. Of many other massive Norman buildings only the names remain, for instance, St. Giles' Hospital, the Malandry, St. Catherine's Priory, and other religious houses. Lincoln was now a busy city. Strangers from many lands trod its narrow streets, but they were not really strangers, for anyone who could speak Latin was a member of that great international society, the Medieval Church, and all who wished to buy or sell, whether Danes or Frisians, Gascons or Lombards, were welcome at Lincoln's quays and wharves. They were fellow citizens of the growing commonwealth of trade. Naturally kings were interested in the city, because kings must have money, and wherever industry and commerce flourish they may expect a rich harvest. In the following chapters let us take a glance at this thriving community, an example of all that was most vigorous and lasting in the life of the middle ages. Let us try to get, if we can, a moving picture of its life and a glimpse of its leading figures as they flit across the screen of history in their monkish cowls, their merchants' robes, their flashing armour, or, now and then, their royal crowns.

CHAPTER V.

FAMOUS BISHOPS.

REMIGIUS.

We must begin with William's Bishop Remigius, "slight in stature, but great in heart ; of dark features, but fair in deeds." He had been the almoner of the monastery at Fécamp in Normandy, and probably could not speak the language of the English and Danes over whom he was set to rule. His diocese was of enormous extent ; it stretched from the Humber to the Thames, and he very naturally wished to build a cathedral which would do honour to the high office which he held. Before the Norman Conquest, the headquarters of the diocese, the seat of the bishop, had been the tiny village of Dorchester, in Oxfordshire. This seems a strange place for the capital of a diocese, until we remember that the early English disliked town life and preferred the tranquility—and the safety—of the countryside. But Remigius, carrying out the wishes of the king, decided to move his see to one of the large towns in his diocese. At some date before 1086, probably between 1072 and 1076, he obtained the king's permission to build his new cathedral at Lincoln, and the document, in which the permission is given, may still be seen in the Cathedral Library.

He selected the site we all know so well—surely one of the most magnificent sites for a cathedral anywhere—and began to build. He built for nearly twenty years. At the very moment that his task was finished, just one day, in fact, before the day fixed for the consecration, he died. His cathedral, of course, was smaller than

West Front of the Norman Cathedral

the one we see today, but if we glance at the picture on page 45 we shall be able to judge what a great achievement the little bishop had accomplished in the last twenty years of his busy life. You will notice too, that the arches are rounded in the usual Norman style, and the pillars and walls are of massive strength, as strong as any castle walls. When we realise that both a castle and a cathedral were built in Lincoln at the same time, and almost side by side, both of unheard-of size and strength, we can imagine the thoughts of the people at Lincoln, especially those whose houses had been swept away to make room for both. These Norman Conquerors were energetic and ruthless. They had evidently come to stay. We can imagine, too, the hammering and clattering, as the English workmen put up the scaffolding for their Norman masters ; the rumbling of country carts as they toiled along the roads with loads of gleaming white limestone from the quarry ; load after load, day after day, year after year for twenty years, with masons and sculptors, brought over from Normandy, bawling orders at the workmen in a language they did not understand. Who paid for it all, and how much did it cost ? It would be interesting to know, but there are no records or accounts to tell us. Yet accounts no doubt were kept, and plans must have been made, too, for huge buildings like this required careful organisation and foresight just as they do today.

Nearly thirty years after the death of Remigius came Alexander, another Norman, who made various additions and alterations to the cathedral, one of which we may still see in the central doorway of the West Front. He was not in such a hurry as Remigius, and could afford to spend more time on ornamentation, as we see by the rich carvings and decorations that surround the doorway.

But the cathedral of Remigius was not destined to survive. Twice it was damaged by fire—one of the worst enemies of medieval towns, owing to the fact, perhaps, that nearly all houses were built of wood, and the only means of lighting was the flaring torch or the guttering candle. The first time was in 1124, when a fire broke out in the timber roof. The roof collapsed. A beam fell on the tomb of Remigius and broke it in two. A tombstone which had been broken in this way was stored for many years in the cloisters, and was believed to be the tombstone of Remigius. In modern times it has been placed in the cathedral a little to the north of the original burial place of Remigius. The body of Remigius had been moved to a tomb in the choir. When the tomb was opened it was found that the Bishop's coffin measured but 51 inches by 16. " Short in stature, but great in heart" said Henry of Huntingdon. In 1185 the cathedral was still further damaged by an earthquake, and in the following year a new bishop was installed who decided to rebuild it entirely in the style we see today.

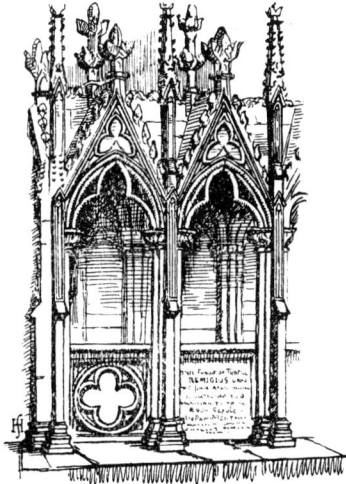

Tomb of Remigius

St. Hugh.

The new bishop was Hugh of Avalon, or, as he later became, St. Hugh. He came from a monastery in the South of France, where he had become famous for his piety and strength of character. His fame reached the ears of Henry II, who was king of half France as well as of England, and knew all the leading men of his time ; and much against his will Hugh was persuaded by Henry to come to England, first as prior of Witham in Somersetshire, and then as bishop of Lincoln. This is another example of the way in which the medieval church in every western European country could draw upon the abilities of men from other lands, no matter of what nationality they might be. St. Hugh, therefore, was more than the Bishop of Lincoln ; he was a great international figure.

He set about reforming the religious life of his diocese and one of his first acts was to insist that a canon should reside near the cathedral, or provide a vicar to carry out his duties. He also began rebuilding the cathedral on an entirely different plan. He began at the east end and built in a style that was almost unknown in England, though it was developing in France. The openings for the doors and windows were pointed and the pillars more graceful. He built the choir in this style, but did not live to finish the whole church. It was continued by his successors, especially by Bishop Grosseteste (1235-53), who for some reason did not pull the whole of the Norman work down, but allowed a part of it to remain, as we see in the West Front, and the new work was built around it. This is very fortunate, as it gives us an idea of the beauty and strength of the earlier building, and enables us to compare the two styles of architecture, the Norman and the Early English, side by side.

Bishop Hugh knew what was right and true and just according to the teachings of the church, and this made him utterly fearless, even in the presence of a tempestuous king like Henry II. He also had as fierce a temper—"hotter and more stinging than pepper," as he himself confessed—but he kept it under control. He had not been at Lincoln very long before he had a violent quarrel with the king over the rights of the church. The king summoned Hugh to his presence to answer for his conduct. Hugh set off, and after much wandering found the king in the forest, where he had been hunting. He was surrounded by his court, who all stood expectantly around waiting for the explosion of the royal wrath. The bishop was received in complete silence ; even his greetings were not answered ; he was obviously in deep disgrace. At last the king sent for a needle and thread and began to stitch a bit of leather round a bandage on his finger. Hugh began to laugh, and remarked "How like your ancestor of Falaise you are !" This was a reference to the fact that Henry was descended from William the Conqueror, whose mother was the daughter of a tanner. The king might have been very angry. Instead he roared with laughter ; he was vastly amused and rolled on the ground in sheer delight, and the quarrel was made up. More than that, the bishop proved he had been right ; he obtained the punishment of his detractors, and took this excellent opportunity of rebuking the king for his unchristian manner of life.

There are many other stories of Bishop Hugh if only we had the space to tell them. There is the famous meeting between the bishop and Richard the Lion Heart, near Rouen in 1198, when the king refused to give the bishop the kiss of peace because he would not supply soldiers to fight in France. The bishop said that the king had no right to demand soldiers for foreign wars, and absolutely refused to supply his quota. In order to settle the matter he determined to meet Richard in person and journeyed to Normandy to seek him out. He found him at La Roche d'Andely where he was taking part in the service of the mass. Hugh boldly went up to him, and, in accordance with the usual practice, demanded the kiss of peace. But the king turned away ; the service was suspended while all watched the duel between two powerful wills. " Kiss me, my lord," said Hugh again, "for I have come far to see thee." " You have not deserved it," replied Richard. " Nay, but I have," and he laid hold of the royal robe, and soundly shook the king, so that he was compelled to look him in the face and give him the kiss of peace. He even rated Richard for various moral offences, and refused to do his bidding. Such was the power of the bishop over the greatest knight in Christendom. He had no illusions in regard to John's feelings towards the church ; and the king's meanness and deceitfulness made him furious. Once when the king stood hesitating whether to put his offering into the alms dish or into his pocket, the bishop's rage boiled over : " Throw it down and go out," he said ; and the king hurriedly threw down his offering and left the church.

There are many other sides to his character that might be touched upon—his love of children, to whom he gave apples and such sweetmeats as were to be had in those days. There is also the story of the swan of Stow which followed him about whenever he went to

Statue on Cathedral said to represent St. Hugh

Stow, and ate out of his hand ; but more important was his careful supervision of his diocese, the reform of the clergy and the rebuilding of the churches that had been allowed to fall into decay. He was a hater of superstition, too, and those who brought wonder working relics to him were sent about their business. Can we wonder that he was revered as a holy man by the common people, and respected even by his enemies ? Two kings attended his funeral, John of England and William of Scotland, and one of the bearers of his coffin was John himself. As the procession, often deep in mud, wended its way up the High Street the citizens threw alms upon the hearse, and as it passed even the Jews joined in the general lamentations. In 1220 he was canonised. No saint in the calendar had won his place more worthily. In 1280 his coffin was deposited in a splendid shrine in the newly built Angel Choir, which was visited by pilgrims from far and wide. They came, not merely to pay tribute to the dead bishop, but to secure the intercession of the saint in the forgiveness of their sins, or the healing of their bodies.

GROSSETESTE.

Thirty-five years after the death of St. Hugh, another bishop came to Lincoln whose name was known in his own lifetime even more widely than St. Hugh's, though he is not so well remembered today. He was Grosseteste—" Great head"—and an Englishman, born of humble parents in Suffolk. Like St. Hugh he vigorously defended the church against its enemies, but unlike St. Hugh, he found them not so much among the kings and the laity, as among the officials of the church itself. He was elected to the see of Lincoln in 1235, and in less than a year he had ordered the removal of no fewer than seven abbots and four priors from the religious houses of his diocese. There can be no doubt that some of the monasteries of his diocese were failing to maintain discipline and enforce their rules, or the bishop would never have had to apply so drastic a remedy.

The bishop also claimed the right to visit (*i.e.*, inspect and correct) the chapter of the cathedral, as he would any religious house in his diocese, and when the canons denied his claim, he suspended the dean, sub-dean and precentor, and appointed a new dean. The canons replied by preaching sermons in the cathedral against the bishop ; the bishop excommunicated the precentor and the chapter excommunicated the new dean. They even went so far as to forge a charter to disprove the bishop's claim to visit them ! And so it went on, until the pope decided in the bishop's favour. The Abbot of Bardney similarly contested the bishop's right to visit and examine the inmates of the abbey, and closed his gates when the visitors appeared. Again the pope was appealed to, and this time he compromised and satisfied neither the bishop nor the abbot. The pace of the bishop was getting too hot for the pope. It soon left him far behind, and Grosseteste did not shrink from expressing his bitter disappointment in a stinging attack on the pope himself.

The cause of the quarrel was the scandalous neglect by a few of the monasteries of the many parish churches they had in their possession. Instead of looking after them as they should, they were content to appoint an underpaid vicar to serve the church and often allowed the buildings to fall into ruins, while they continued to draw the tithes and other revenues. In the eyes of Grosseteste, this was a scandalous neglect of duty on the part of these monasteries. He insisted that vicars should be appointed with a right to a definite income, usually one-third of the revenues of the church, and that they should not be liable to be dismissed. He determined to compel the neglectful monks to surrender their rights. He obtained letters from the pope to enable him to enforce their surrender, but the monks took the case to Rome, and though Grosseteste appeared and defended his cause in person, the decision went against him. Thus the pope went back on his word, because, it is thought, the monasteries were rich and able to bribe him, and Grosseteste returned bitterly disappointed. He had further cause for anger when the pope wished him to find a canonry for an ignorant Italian, and another for the pope's nephew. The bishop refused them both, and as a punishment for his courage and honesty, he was suspended from his office. Grosseteste supported the pope's authority when properly used, but objected to the abuse of his power.

Grosseteste was equally severe on the sins of the laity. Like the puritans of the 17th century, he deeply suspected the games and the dancing and merrymaking that went on at holiday times in the villages. They led to drunkenness, bloodshed and every kind of wickedness, he thought—and he ordered his vicars and rectors to put down village games and processions. If we could see the way in which they were carried out we should probably agree that he was right ! He also opposed the extravagant and futile policy of Henry III. But Grosseteste's most lasting work was in another sphere. Great reformer as he was, he was greater still as a scholar and scientist. He was one of the few people who believed that in order to understand the Bible properly it was necessary to study the languages in which it was first written, and this of course meant that he must know Hebrew and Greek as well as Latin. He also believed that men should observe nature. He tried many scientific experiments, and the superstitious people of the time came to look upon him as a sorcerer. If only he had obtained more widespread support he might have brought about great reforms in the church. He had a great disciple, Roger Bacon, who experimented with lenses and is said to have invented gunpowder ; but, like his master, he had to wage continual war against the prejudice and ignorance of his superiors, and when he died his work was forgotten for centuries.

Grosseteste was the greatest of the medieval bishops of Lincoln, but there were many other notable figures and events during this period, and to these we must now turn.

CHAPTER VI.

RED LETTER DAYS.

THE TRIAL OF THE TEMPLARS.

First we must tell the story of the Knights Templars. In 1309 occurred one of the most dramatic events in the long and interesting history of the city. A court was called in the chapter house of the cathedral, presided over by the bishop, to try the proud and fearless Templars whose Preceptory at Temple Bruer, ten miles to the south of Lincoln, had stood for more than a hundred years. In 1308 they had been suddenly and secretly arrested by the express order of the king, and they were now brought to trial on charges of which many are too horrible to believe, though some are apparently supported by the finds that were made more than five hundred years later when the vaults of their Preceptory were opened by excavators.

The Knights Templars had formed their order during the crusades, when these knights bound themselves by solemn vow to devote their lives to the protection of pilgrims in the Holy Land. They lived near the Temple in Jerusalem and so became known as the Knights of the Temple, or the Templars. Their order grew rapidly, and Preceptories, in which they lived, were founded in all parts of western Europe. One of them was established outside Lincoln about 1185 at Temple Bruer, where a tower still stands to mark the spot, and a small town sprang up around the church and buildings of the Preceptory. Charters were obtained for a weekly market and an annual fair was held. No doubt the townspeople of

Lincoln flocked to the annual tournaments that were held by the Templars on the heath, at which the knights would challenge all comers, and no doubt held their own.

The order continued to flourish and its wealth to increase for over a hundred years ; and then, at the beginning of the 14th century, attacks were made upon them in every country in Europe. They had deeply offended the King of France, who became their bitter enemy ; the pope, Clement V, who was jealous of the Templars and a great friend of the French king, was willing to lend his aid ; and the two of them conspired to bring about the downfall of the rich and powerful order. The Templars were suddenly accused of terrible crimes—murder, blasphemy, the slaughter of infants. The pope ordered immediate investigation in all the countries of Christendom, including, of course, England. Special courts were appointed at London, York and Lincoln to try the accused men.

It was necessary to go about the business carefully. The Templars were rich and powerful and might be expected to make a fight of it if they were given warning of their impending fate. In order to prevent this, the king sent secret and special instructions to the sheriff of Lincolnshire by one of the Clerks of the Council. But before reading them he was required to take a solemn oath that he would obey the orders without question, whatever they were, and not reveal them to anyone. He was to summon twelve trusty men to execute the order, who were also to take an oath of secrecy.

When the instructions were read, it was found that the sheriff and his twelve men were to arrest all the Knights Templars in his Baili-wick ; to seize in the name of the king, all the lands, goods, tenements, chattels, charters, writings and muniments, to make an inventory of them, and to keep the knights themselves in safe custody— though not in a "strait or loathsome prison"—until they should be

Gatehouse at the eastern end of Clasketgate.
Demolished 1786

brought to trial. Some of the Templars were kept in the gatehouse at the eastern end of Clasketgate.

The court met in 1309, but the trial was transferred to London. The more serious charges were not proved, but some of the knights were found guilty of minor offences, and the Order was suppressed.

JOHN OF GAUNT.

An event which would arouse much interest among Lincoln citizens was the marriage of John of Gaunt and Katharine Swynford that took place in the cathedral in 1396, almost ninety years after the trial of the Templars. John of Gaunt had been married twice before. His first wife was Blanche, the daughter of the Duke of Lancaster, and it was through her that he acquired his title of Earl of Lincoln, among his many other titles, and also the possession of the castle of Lincoln. Blanche died of plague, and John took as his second wife Constance, the daughter of the King of Castile ; and when she died in 1394, he married Katharine Swynford, widow of the Lincolnshire knight, Sir Hugh Swynford of Kettlethorpe, and the sister-in-law of the famous poet Geoffrey Chaucer.

John of Gaunt is said to have built a mansion for Katharine on the west side of High Street to the north of St. Mary's Guild

The story of this period has been well told by Anya Seton in her novel "Katherine" published in 1954.

Hall, in order to provide a warmer and more sheltered home for her and her children than the old Norman castle. If he did this, there is no written evidence to prove that the house known as "John of Gaunt's Palace" was really his mansion. A picture of the house drawn in 1726 shows it to have been a very handsome

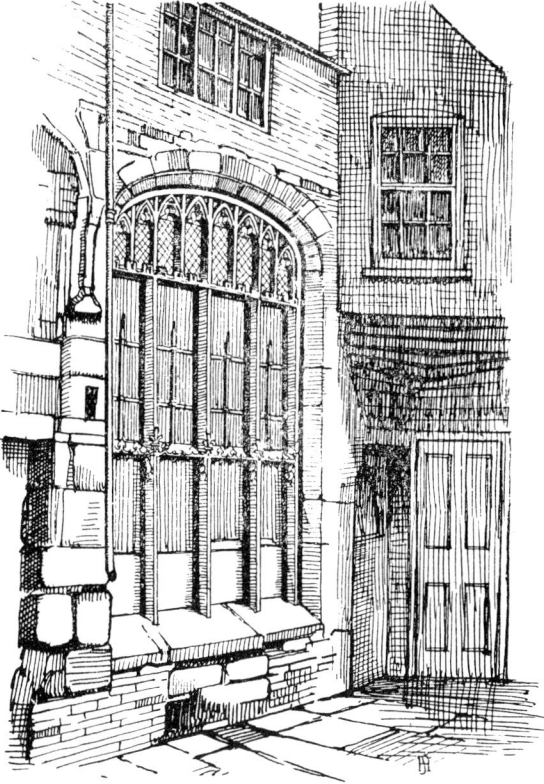

Remains of " John of Gaunt's Palace"

building in perpendicular style with a brave show of buttresses, battlements and pinnacles. Part of one room, with a fine window, is now built into the back premises of No. 117 High Street, and a fine oriel window from the palace has been placed in the wall of the lodge on the north side of the entrance to the castle. Katharine Swynford lived at Lincoln, or at Kettlethorpe, until her death in 1403, and her tomb, and that of her daughter Joan, the grandmother of the Earl of Warwick, the Kingmaker, may still be seen in the cathedral.

ROYAL VISITS.

But the most spectacular, though perhaps not the most welcome, of the sights that greeted the eyes of Lincoln citizens were the visits of kings and their advisers in the course of their perpetual movement about the royal dominions. King Stephen, as we have seen, must have been a familiar and by no means welcome figure to the citizens of Lincoln during his disastrous wars with Matilda. His successor, Henry II, spent Christmas here in 1158, and to make sure of the loyalty of the northern counties, had himself crowned a second time. For some reason, the ceremony took place in Wigford outside the city walls, possibly because of the old belief that a king who wore his crown in Lincoln would never prosper. Certainly the superstitious could point to the sad case of Stephen, who had worn his crown when he spent the Christmas of 1147 at Lincoln and no good had come of it ! Henry II was fairly generous to Lincoln in the way of charters and privileges, much more so than he was to London, but in return the city had to pay dearly in increased taxes as we shall see ; and *somebody* must have been the poorer for his stay in the city, for no fewer than twenty tuns of wine, a hundred wooden cups, a hundred pounds of wax, sixty pounds of pepper and three hundred scullions were sent by the sheriffs of London, while the sheriffs of six neighbouring counties kept him supplied with venison.

The window at 117 High Street was removed in 1963 and is stored awaiting re-erection in a medieval museum.

No doubt the merchants and craftsmen and alehouse keepers did a roaring trade that Christmas ; but perhaps the sheriff of Lincolnshire was glad when it was all over, since he had to pay the expenses of repairing the royal house and finding quarters for the royal hunstmen and their squires.

King John was the most expensive of all the royal visitors. He spent much time in the city in 1200 and 1201, and helped to carry the coffin of St. Hugh up the Steep, as we have seen. He also renewed the city's charters and liberties ; but for these royal favours he had to be paid—seven hundred marks and seven palfreys and another 500 marks in 1212. No wonder the city fathers took the side of the Barons at Runnymede. But their troubles were by no means over. John came again in 1216 and demanded no fewer than 1,000 marks. It was impossible to find such a large sum, so John took a number of leading citizens as hostages until the money should be paid. Does this help to explain why Prince Louis took refuge in Lincoln when he found himself deserted by the Barons after John's death ? At any rate, such exactions by the king help us to understand the movement that took place in the next reign for control, through parliament, of the power of the king.

Probably one of the most spectacular royal visits was in 1280, when Edward I took part

By courtesy of] [E. J. Burrow and Co., Ltd.

Statues of Edward I and Eleanor

in the ceremony of moving the remains of St. Hugh to the new shrine which had been built for him in the beautiful Angel Choir that had just been opened. St Hugh's tomb had become so famous for its miracles and such a favourite meeting place of pilgrims that it had been decided to find a more worthy resting place for such distinguished—and profitable—remains. A splendid extension of the chancel eastwards was planned—and in order to carry it out it was necessary to make a breach in the city walls, for which permission was obtained from the king in 1255. The world famous Angel Choir was the result.

The idea of church architecture had altered considerably since St. Hugh introduced the new style. If we stand where the two choirs meet, we shall see that the masonry of the Angel Choir is much more ornamental than that of St. Hugh's. The capitals of the pillars are more elaborately carved ; the mouldings are richer ; and the spaces in the triangles between the arches in the triforium arcade are filled by carvings of angels, which gives the name of "Angel Choir" to this part of the cathedral. It is a splendid example of what is known as the " Decorated Style."

It would be interesting to know who did the actual work of building this masterpiece. Was the carving of all those angels, each with a character and expression of its own, done by a sculptor on the spot, or were the angels ordered by the architect in charge from some well known sculptor's workshop in London or elsewhere and merely "assembled" by the masons at Lincoln ? If a careful examination is made of photographs of the different figures it will be seen that though the carving is first-class throughout, there has been some error in fitting one or two of the figures into their panels. It is hardly likely that this would have happened if the whole work had been done on the spot under the eye of the skilled craftsmen who did the carving. Ten years after the opening of the

Angel Choir, King Edward visited Lincoln again. This time his errand was a sad one. He was bringing with him the body of his beloved wife, Eleanor, to her last resting place in Westminster.

PARLIAMENTS.

In 1301 the king was here again, in connection with a meeting of parliament that had been arranged at Lincoln so that Edward should be able to attend to the business of the country while at the same time supervising the preparations for his war with Scotland. Altogether three hundred people met, representing the barons, the church, the law and the universities, but not the towns, since the business was mainly concerned with the claims of the pope and the administration of the forests. Many preparations were necessary for so important an assembly and the sheriff of Lincoln received orders to provide corn and hay for four hundred horses for a month, and a hundred beeves and three hundred sheep were to be well salted and placed in the larder ready for the meeting. To ensure that proper records should be taken of the proceedings, the sheriff was also ordered to procure sixty dozens of good parchment for the use of the clerks.

The parliament met in the chapter house of the cathedral, and the fine old oak chair, with lions on the armrests, which still stands there, may have been made for this great occasion. The king found parliament willing to support him against the extravagant

Chair in the Chapter House
(without modern canopy)

claims of the pope, Boniface VIII, but when he went on to deal with questions concerning the royal forests, he was met with obstruction. Parliament was very anxious to get the royal forests properly surveyed, and the powers of the royal officers of the forests properly defined. We should remember that the royal forests at this time covered a very large part of England. They were administered by royal officers, who were subject to the king alone, and could not be punished in the ordinary law courts however oppressive they might be, and since many of them had obtained their offices by bribery, they were inclined to impose extortionate fines for breaches of the forest laws. At the same time, the rich barons were anxious to curtail the royal forests as much as possible so that they might add to their own domains. If only the king would grant parliament's wishes in regard to the forests they would increase the taxes recently granted by 20 per cent! Evidently the royal forests were a very serious matter to the parliament of 1301.

The king's accounts dealing with the expenses of this parliament give us some interesting information. The sheriff's bills for food, firewood, coal, salt, and hay amounted to £750, and during the eleven days that parliament had sat, the members had drunk 3,121 gallons of ale at a penny a gallon—that is a gallon a day each. We also learn that oxen cost two marks (26s. 8d.) ; pigs 2—4 shillings ; sheep 1s. 6d. ; wheat was 4s. a quarter ; malt 3s. 2d. ; and a good horse cost £3 6s. 8d., but it was possible to get one for 10s.

Lincoln witnessed another parliament in January, 1316, which was mainly notable for a brawl between the king's favourite, Despencer, and one of the "opposition" barons. This parliament used the Dean's Hall and the great hall of the White Friars for some of its meetings, as well as the Chapter House. In July, 1316, and in 1327, other parliaments were held in Lincoln.

LATER ROYAL VISITS.

There were many more royal visits to this ancient and important centre, one of the keys to the northern parts of the king's dominions. Edward III came three times in the period 1328 to 1331 ; Richard II and his queen came in 1387, and it is probably in consequence of this visit that the mayor has the right to have a sword carried before him on civic occasions. In 1445, Henry VI and Margaret visited the city and received a present of £100 in gold, a very handsome gift considering the poor state of the town at this time. Possibly the city fathers were hoping to make it up by getting a reduction of taxes, for two years later they petitioned the king to reduce the burden owing to their great impoverishment following upon a visitation of the pestilence and other misfortunes. When Edward IV visited the city in 1461 on his way to the battle of Towton, the impoverished city could do no more than make him a present for his table ; it consisted of twelve pike, twelve tench, and twelve bream. One wonders if poverty was the only reason for so poor a gift. Henry VII also received a gift of fish for his table, including a dozen salmon as well as the more commonplace tench and pike. And in a similarly humble spirit, Henry VII, in accordance with the custom of the times, washed the feet of thirty poor men on the Thursday before Good Friday (Maundy-

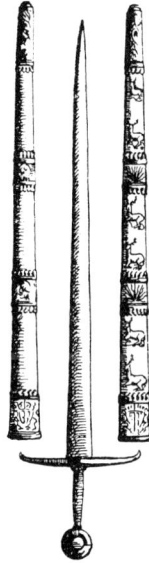

The Sword of
Richard II

Thursday) in the bishop's hall. He distributed alms generously, and seems to have won popularity with the people, for when he came again in 1487, after his victory at Stoke, he was welcomed joyously, and presented with a gift of twelve fat oxen, a score of fat sheep and "six gret fat pikes" for his table.

Much more elaborate preparations were felt necessary for the visit of King Henry VIII. He had just triumphed over the rebellious peasants of Lincolnshire and Yorkshire in the Pilgrimage of Grace, and perhaps it was felt that special precautions should be taken to avoid rousing his imperious temper. Not only did the city fathers make him a lavish grant of oxen, sheep and fish ; they ordered the citizens to carry away within two days "all dunghills, gravel, stone, and other like stuff now lying in the city," and to sprinkle loads of sand in the streets against the king's coming. The king was to be met at the city boundary and every alderman who had been mayor was to have a scarlet gown, and every other alderman a crimson one and all the inhabitants 'of ability' to make themselves gowns of London russet or other like colour. The royal visitors dined at Temple Bruer, and then, before meeting the city fathers, they changed their clothes in the tents provided for them, the king into cloth of gold, the queen (Catherine Howard, his fifth wife) into cloth of silver, and so the gay show passed through the sanded streets, with the mayor bearing the city mace, Lord Hastings the king's sword, and the aldermen in their scarlet and crimson and the citizens in their London russet, until they reached the bishop's palace. But tragedy swiftly followed in its wake, for the next thing the citizens of Lincoln heard was that the queen had been accused of treason committed during her stay in Lincoln and was on trial for her life. Here was a skeleton at the feast indeed !

What kind of a place was the bishop's hall in which these brilliant scenes—and dark intrigues—were enacted ? It was built by Bishop Hugh in the twelfth century, and had a large middle aisle with smaller aisles on either side, and light grey pillars of Purbeck marble to support the arched roof. From the upper halves of the richly painted windows, the kings of England looked down on the guests ;

Photograph by)

THE JEWS' HOUSE AND THE JEWS' COURT

(J. Dixon Scott

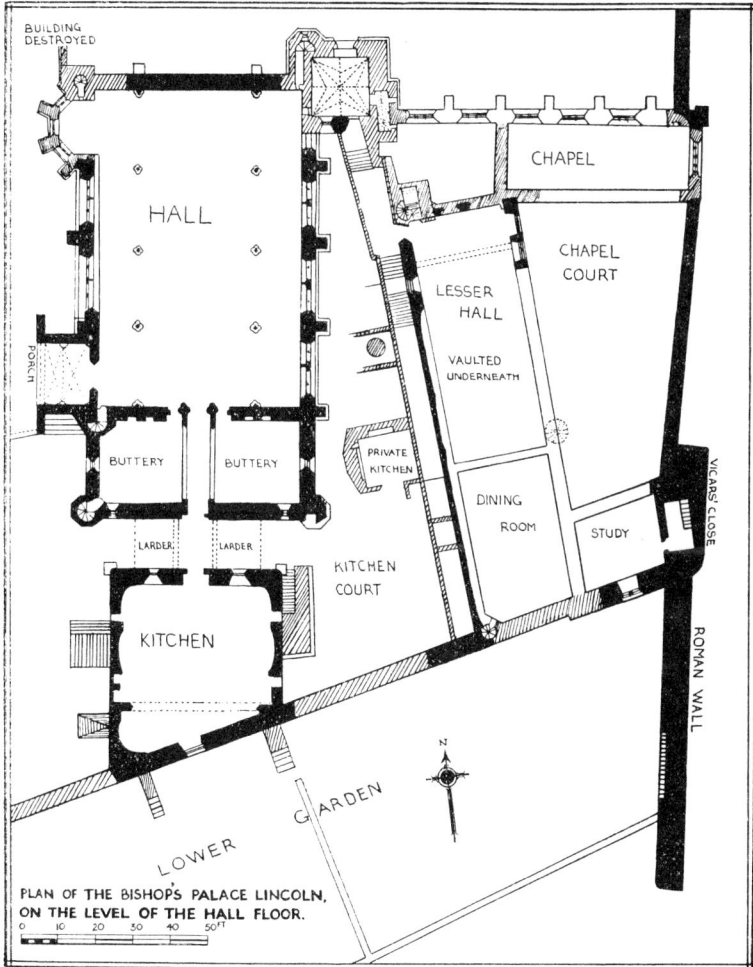

Plan of the Ruins of the Old Bishop's Palace

the lower lights were open except for wooden shutters, which could be closed at night or in bad weather.

In early times the life of the palace centred round this great hall. Like other lords, the bishop had many residences, and visited them all at intervals, taking with him numerous followers. The produce of his lands and manors was stored up to await his coming and when it was exhausted he moved on. No doubt the bishop's manor of Nettleham supplied some of his needs when at Lincoln. In preparation for his arrival the great hall would be hung with tapestries, and for the time being it would become almost a public room. There the household lived during the day and slept at night. But the bishop could retire to a chamber on the first floor at the southern end of the hall when he wished for privacy and freedom from the throng of his followers and visitors. Beneath this chamber was a passage leading to the great kitchen, and on each side of the passage were butteries and larders, and below was the principal cellar. The kitchen had five huge fireplaces. An additional wing, containing a smaller hall and dining room, had been built by Bishop Alnwick. To live in such princely style the bishop required enormous revenues, but in the sixteenth century the power of the church declined and he found himself unable to keep up his magnificent state. Bishop Longland, who entertained Henry VIII, as we have seen above, was the last of the wealthy bishops, and it may be that the king cast envious eyes on the revenues which provided hin with such lavish entertainment. Whatever the cause, his successor had to surrender most of the episcopal estates. He left the palace and went to live at his manor house at Nettleham. During the civil wars the palace was burnt, as we shall see in another chapter. The lead was stripped from the roof and the palace fell into ruin. It was used as a quarry from which to repair the cathedral ; but in 1885 a part of it was restored and enlarged and from 1888 to 1945 it was again the home of the bishops of Lincoln. The ruins of the old palace form one of the most picturesque and impressive sights of the city.

There was one occasion between the visit of Henry VIII and the destruction of the civil wars on which the bishop's hall returned to its former gaiety and splendour. That was when King James I paid his memorable visit in 1617. The two sheriffs and the chief citizens had arranged to meet him on the road from Grantham, but the king preferred to hunt along the heath rather than follow the highway, so they missed him and had to come back to Lincoln and prepare to meet him near the Cross on the Cliff 'where his Majesty could not miss them.' Here they stood two by two in rank, the sheriffs in purple gowns with white staffs in their hands, the chamberlains in violet, the chief citizens in black gowns, all booted and spurred on their horses with new javelins in their hands, fringed with red and white, and as the king's coach drew near, the elder sheriff, kneeling before the king, delivered his staff, which was given back to him, and the other sheriff did the like, and thus both rode bareheaded before the coach, and so with a flourish of trumpets, hautboys, and drums, and the music of the city waits, they brought the royal visitor to St. Catherine's. The next day the king visited the cathedral ; the recorder made a speech—a short one "for the king had no love of long speeches"—the mayor presented a silver gilt cup ; the dean said prayers in the cathedral before the whole assembly and the king returned with all the pomp and acclamation that Lincoln could provide, to his lodgings at St. Catherine's. Next day, being Sunday, he went once more to the cathedral and after the sermon was ended, he healed no fewer than fifty persons suffering from the King's Evil, and on the following Tuesday another fifty-three ! On the Sunday he had dined at the palace with Bishop Neile.

The Old Palace has been taken into guardianship by the Department of the Environment and extensive restoration carried out. It will shortly be open to the public.

After this good work the king felt he was entitled to his pleasures, for on Wednesday he came to the George Hotel, by the Stonebow, to see a cocking, where four cocks were put in the pit together "which made his Majesty very merry." And then to the Spread Eagle, where there was a fencing match between the scholars of the city and some of the strong men of the court, in which there were broken pates and other hurts, but the scholars had the better of it ; and on the Thursday there was a great horse race on the heath for a cup presented by the king, and another between three Irishmen and an Englishman. The course was a quarter of a mile long and was railed off with ropes and stoops, whereby the people were kept out and "the horses which ronned were seen far." On the Saturday he left for Newark, thanking the citizens for their welcome, and saying that if God gave him life he would see them oftener. Thus ended one of the most memorable royal visits in Lincoln history.

Charles I came, as we shall see, under less carefree circumstances, and in October 1695 William III passed through Lincoln on his way from Grantham to Welbeck. The sheriffs and their officers rode up Cross-o'-Cliff Hill to meet the king's coach, and at 7 o'clock, after their weary wait in the dark, the king arrived.

Torches, links and flamboys lighted the way to the Great Bargate where the mayor, recorder, aldermen and citizens were waiting to welcome the king. From the Great Bargate the mayor, wearing the hat of maintenance on his head, carried the sword before the king's coach up the High Street to the king's lodgings at Lieutenant Colonel Pownall's house, which now forms Nos. 4 and 5 Pottergate. The procession included the aldermen on horseback, the Lincoln and Newark waits or minstrels, local gentlemen and citizens, and about 70 nobles and gentlemen who had come with the king. They rode along with music playing, trumpets sounding, drums beating and bells ringing. The streets were illuminated and crowded with vast numbers of people shouting and cheering. Candles also burned brightly in the windows of all houses and shops.

That night the city officials were entertained at a banquet at the king's lodgings with "wine of all sorts and sweetmeats in great quantities, all at the king's charge." But the visit was only a passing call. By 7 o'clock the next morning the king was preparing to leave the city, and after hearing prayers in the Minster he continued his journey, leaving Lincoln to settle down again to the sleepy life of a country market town.

But our story has hurried along too quickly, and we must retrace our steps to look a little more closely at the lives of the people who lived in this city during the middle ages.

CHAPTER VII.

LINCOLN IN THE MIDDLE AGES.

How Lincoln was Governed.

At the present time the city is governed by a council consisting of a mayor and aldermen and a number of councillors elected by the inhabitants of the different wards into which the city is divided. The office of mayor goes back to 1206, but the division of the city into smaller units for the purposes of government goes back even further. Under Henry II (1154-89) there were already four wards in the city, and earlier still, before the Norman Conquest, the city was ruled by twelve hereditary lawmen (probably the chief land-owners) who held courts for their tenants, kept the peace, and sometimes sat together to "give the law" to the whole town.

When the Normans came, the government of the city was gradually changed. The new king, William the Conqueror, was afraid that the conquered English and Danes might rebel, and also that the barons he had brought with him might become too strong, and so he wished to keep as much power as possible in his own hands. Instead of the hereditary lawmen, the sheriff of the county—an officer appointed by the king—took over the government of the city. He came at regular intervals to hold a court, collect the taxes and keep the peace in the king's name. Even the bishop had to pay a rent for some of the lands he held of the king, not a large rent—it consisted of a rich cloak trimmed with sables—but it was a recognition of the king's rights over his lands. The city itself had to pay a substantial sum in hard cash—£140 a year (equal to a very large sum today), the " Farm " of the city as it was called—and if the sheriff could squeeze any more for himself, he did !

For sixty years and more this went on, and no doubt the rich merchants and landowners of Lincoln were very tired of the sheriff's exactions and interference in their affairs, but in 1130, in return for an increased " Farm", the king allowed the city to rule itself once more. In place of the county sheriff (or Shire-reeve) the city was allowed to appoint a reeve of its own, who should be pleasing to the chief citizens and also to the king.

This must have been a very valuable privilege, for Lincoln promised to pay the king £40 more than it had paid to the sheriff. Evidently Lincoln was recovering her prosperity as well as her independence, otherwise she would not have shouldered so heavy a burden. One reason for this was that the city had been given very important privileges by the Norman kings, amounting practically to a monopoly of the foreign trade in the whole of Lincolnshire, and it should be remembered that the Norman kings were in a position not only to grant, but to enforce privileges of this kind, and Lincoln owed much of her prosperity to this, as we shall find.

All through the Danish period the trade of the city had been growing, especially with Scandinavia, and even after the set-back of the Norman Conquest there were still many merchants at the time of the Domesday enquiry. They were organised in a Merchants' Gild, which no doubt had a good deal to do with the collection of the " Farm" of the city, and, after 1130, with the election of the reeve. But besides the merchants who lived at Lincoln, many foreign traders came to buy and sell. In fact, all foreigners trading with Lincolnshire ports were compelled by the king to come to Lincoln to pay tolls on the goods they brought into, or took out of the county. This must have been very inconvenient to the merchants who might wish to trade in other towns in Lincolnshire, but it was useful to the kings whose officers could keep watch on the payment of tolls in one place like Lincoln much better than in a large number of places, and for Lincoln it was a boon. The foreign merchants came, grumbling no doubt—but to the members of the Merchant Gild of Lincoln, who alone had the right of trading in the market with foreigners, the arrangement was invaluable. Not only did it bring foreign merchants with their wares to the city, but it attracted all the merchants of Lincolnshire—from Louth, Boston, Grimsby and other towns—to buy from them. Thus Lincoln became a great centre of exchange. Merchants from Scandinavia and Germany with their furs, iron, alum, amber and gums, and from France and the Mediterranean countries, with their spices, wines, silks and jewels, met here to buy Lincolnshire wool, hides, leather and possibly corn, for the towns of Flanders and Italy.

It should be remembered too, that all the merchants who came to trade in Lincoln had to pay a share of the city's taxes, that is to say, they had to become members of the Merchant Gild and pay their share of the city's " Farm" to the king just as though they were resident citizens. Now we can see how Lincoln could afford to pay another £40 a year to the king for the privilege of ruling itself and getting rid of the sheriff. But they had set themselves a big task. They had undertaken to do the sheriff's work, to keep the peace of the city, to collect the tolls and to hand over every year to the king's exchequer a sum of £180. In 1200 they added further to

Figure on Cathedral showing
medieval costume

their burdens in order to obtain additional " liberties." They were allowed to elect two of the more lawful and discreet citizens as reeves, and for this they had to pay the large sum of 300 marks (£200. 1 mark=13s. 4d.). In 1210 they paid a further £100 for the right of electing a mayor and two reeves or bailiffs, though sometimes the mayor was also one of the bailiffs. But the price of these privileges was high and if, as Dr. Coulton tells us, we should multiply figures of an even later date by 40 in order to get modern equivalents, there is no wonder that the citizens guarded their charters so jealously and exacted tolls from all comers, Lincolnshire men and foreigners alike.

No wonder, too, there was grumbling by other Lincolnshire towns, and not only grumbling, but smuggling. Why should the men of Boston and Louth, Sleaford and Grimsby, come all the way to Lincoln to do their trading ? Why should the foreign merchants not be allowed to trade in other Lincolnshire towns ? But the king had given these privileges to Lincoln alone in return for heavy payments. They were laid down solemnly in letters and charters, and Lincoln did her best to enforce them. In 1262 the king himself had to issue a solemn warning about smuggling. The lay brethren of the neighbouring monasteries, it was said, were in the habit of buying up small parcels of wool and selling them to foreigners outside Lincoln, and so avoiding the payment of tolls "whereby the customs of the king are fraudulently withdrawn." To prevent these breaches of the rules, the city appointed inspectors who had to swear solemnly not to allow any foreign merchants to trade outside the city, but the men of Louth and Sleaford said they had a perfect right to trade anywhere in the county, and they absolutely refused to contribute to the "gelds" and customs (*i.e.*, taxes and tolls) of the Lincoln Merchant Gild. In consequence, whenever a merchant from Louth or Sleaford came to Lincoln, he was in danger of having his goods seized by the mayor's officers as payment to the Lincoln Gild. In fact, the mayor actually went to Boston and arrested two men there himself, on the grounds that they owed taxes to the Lincoln Gild. He also seized the horses and the money of Grimsby merchants for the same reason. Lincoln could hardly have been popular with its neighbours in those days !

As long as the carriage of imports and exports was mainly in the hands of foreigners the struggle went on, but little by little English merchants began to own ships. They began to transport their own goods, not only from one market to another, but also to foreign markets abroad. Such towns as Grimsby and Boston—especially Boston—began to grow at the expense of Lincoln, and it became impossible to compel merchants to come to Lincoln to do their trading. Gradually the charters ceased to be enforced although they were never revoked. New centres of foreign trade sprang up which acquired privileges of their own, and from about 1350 Lincoln lost her monopoly, and gradually ceased—on this ground at any rate—to quarrel with her neighbours.

But the rulers of Lincoln were faced with other problems. As we have seen, the city was allowed to govern itself through its own officers, the mayor and bailiffs, in place of the king's sheriff, but this does not mean that the city was at the end of its troubles. On the contrary, this arrangement marked the beginning of new difficulties, for it raised (as we might expect) the question of who had the right of choosing the civic officers and what was to be done if they abused their powers.

Let us stop for a moment to enquire what we mean when we say "the city ruled itself." Do we mean that all the citizens took part ? That they sat on councils and committees as our representatives do now ? Lincoln had about 5,000 inhabitants, so it would not have been impossible for all the heads of families—one thousand people perhaps—to share in the conduct of local affairs. But this does not seem to have been the case. The right of electing the officers was vested in the "chief citizens"—landowners and merchants—who formed the "common counsel" of the city, and there was often bitter dispute between them and the poorer classes, who were excluded. In 1267 for instance, "the commons," as the ordinary people were called, as distinct from the group of leading citizens, the "common counsel" who ruled the city, complained that they had been compelled to pay extortionate prices for the privilege of citizenship, *e.g.*, the right of buying and selling in the market, and that the borough court, to which they were entitled as citizens to bring their cases, only met twice or thrice a year instead of every week ; and also that taxes were being misappropriated and that no account had been rendered of the city's finances. As a result of the common counsel's misgovernment, they said, the city had already been twice taken back into the king's hands as a punishment, and the authority of the sheriff restored. In 1290 the same thing happened again, and on this occasion we know a little more about the causes of the dispute, which were very interesting. It seems that the quarrels between rich and poor had continued. The poor complained that their taxes had not been properly assessed and (probably in lieu of taxation) their fishing nets had been seized by the rich. But there was a more serious grievance and it was this. When the king had expelled the Jews in 1290 he ordered that their property should be given up to him, but a part of it had been kept back, and so the king levied a fine of 200 marks upon the city as a punishment. But instead of obtaining this from those who had pocketed the property of the Jews, the city authorities placed the burden upon everybody, including the poor, and those who would not pay had their property seized and sold. A bitter quarrel naturally broke out, and as a punishment for its failure to manage its affairs more satisfactorily the king took the government of the city into his own hands and ruled it for ten years through his own nominee.

After that it was decided that some better system must be devised for governing the city, and about 1300 it was agreed that the mayors should be assisted by 12 aldermen and four treasurers or chamberlains, one of the four to each ward into which the city was divided at this time. There was also to be an officer in charge of the weighing machine to see that fair measure was weighed out to those who bought and sold wool, hides and other merchandise in the city market. In each parish there were to be two constables, and the chamberlains of the wards were to have the custody of the profits or tolls and tallages. Whether this met the desires of the "commonalty" of Lincoln is somewhat doubtful, as they were still excluded from a share in the election of the mayor and bailiffs. The chief power remained with a small group of wealthy merchants, but though there were further disputes, as we shall see, they never resulted in the city losing its rights of self-government, and being handed over once more to the sheriff of the county.

CHAPTER VIII.

THE JEWS IN LINCOLN.

We must now turn to the subject of the Jews, whose expulsion gave rise to such a tumult in 1290. They had begun to settle in Lincoln in the time of Stephen, attracted by the extensive trade that was being done there, and also by the fact that there was a royal castle to which they might look for protection. In the peaceful reign of Henry II they had gradually grown to be one of the richest and most famous Jewries in England, second only, in number, to that of London, and kings, abbots, earls, knights and merchants, had all been in their debt.

The most famous of all the Lincoln Jews was Aaron, one of the men "behind the scenes" in the reign of Henry II. He did business under the king's protection in nine shires, and when he died he was so rich that the king (who could always seize the Jews' property when they died) had to open a special branch of the exchequer, with two treasurers and two clerks, to wind up his affairs. The debts owing to him were, alone, worth £20,000, which was more than half the yearly income of the king, and Henry II was the greatest king in Christendom at that time. Aaron had agents in Norfolk, Yorkshire, Cambridge, Oxford, Rutland and Buckinghamshire, and was closely connected with the head of the Jewish community in London. With him worked his two brothers Senior and Benedict, and his three sons, Elias, Abraham and Vives. He helped to provide the money for the conquest of Ireland by Strongbow, and for building sixteen monasteries and cathedrals, including Lincoln and Peterborough, and the abbeys of Kirkstead, Louth

Park and Revesby. The Archbishop of Canterbury was among his borrowers, and the ornaments of Lincoln cathedral were pledged to him for the money he lent for building it. He was also a dealer in hay and corn. Altogether 90 abbeys, manors and large houses are known to have been pledged to the Jews in the twelfth century, and of these 45 were pledged to Aaron.

The House of Aaron

The house which unsupported tradition asserts that he occupied can still be seen on the Steep Hill, adjoining the wall of the Bail. Apart from the cathedral and the castle, it was one of the most substantial buildings in Lincoln. Other Jews' houses were near by,

It is now clear (Hill, J. W. F. *Medieval Lincoln*, 1948) that Aaron lived within the Bail and not outside the south gate.

and it used to be thought that they formed a Jews' quarter or ghetto in which only the Jews lived. It was supposed to reach down to the end of the Strait and have a barrier at the bottom, called Dern-stall Lock, which was closed at sunset to prevent anyone from going in or out. But this is certainly wrong. At the time we are speaking of, ghettos were almost unknown in Europe and the Jews mixed freely with their Christian neighbours as they do in most countries today. The " Jews' House" and the " Jews' Court" can still be seen in the Strait, and they date from this period. The ground floors of these Norman houses were used as store rooms, and were fitted, not with windows, but with loop holes. The windows you can see today were inserted at a much later date. On the floor above were the living rooms, which for some reason had fireplaces over the lower doorways. It is possible that one of their buildings, the Jews' Court, built about 1175, was used either as a synagogue or a school, or both. The daily business of the Jews required a good education. Subjects such as arithmetic, medical science and also the Hebrew and Arabic languages were studied. Their schools were the best in England, and were often attended by Christian pupils who wished to share the learning of the Jewish Rabbis, which was much wider than that of the average churchman.

At first the Jews were allowed to live in peace, but as time went on they became more and more unpopular, and every man's hand was turned against them. This was partly due to the influence of the crusades which became especially powerful in the reign of Richard the Lion Heart, and at his coronation in 1189 there was a terrible outbreak against them in London and many were massacred. In Lincoln, too, an attack upon them was planned, but they had wisely taken refuge with the constable of the castle, who protected them and their belongings from the mob.

Another reason for their unpopularity was the heavy rate of interest they charged upon their loans. It was nearly always more than 20 per cent per annum and sometimes as much as 100 per cent. Aaron's rate varied from 1d. to 4d. per pound per week, that is, from 20 per cent to 80 per cent per annum, and you may be sure that many of his borrowers were utterly ruined.

It should be remembered that Christians were not allowed to practise usury, and if they lent any money, they were forbidden by the church to receive anything by way of interest. But these prohibitions did not extend to the Jews, and consequently, whenever large sums of money were wanted for building a castle, or a monastery, or for equipping a knight for the crusades, or for commercial dealings of any kind, it was to the Jews that the borrower usually went. Churchmen as well as laymen borrowed from them, and it is difficult to see how the great buildings of the middle ages, such as cathedrals, castles and monasteries, could have been set up without their aid. And of course, they were a source of wealth to the king. According to the law, all the Jews and everything they had belonged to the king, so that he could levy taxes and fines on them whenever he liked, and, by another law, the goods of a usurer were forfeit to the king when he died. Consequently on the death of a Jew, the whole of his property, including the debts which were owed to him, passed to the king. The Jews were no better off if they became converted to Christianity, since by a law of Henry II, they had to forfeit their property to the king to compensate him for all they *would* have left at their death if they had remained Jews ! Eventually the king agreed to take only half. By another law of Henry II, the famous Assize of Arms, they were forbidden to have either arms or armour to defend themselves in case of attack. They were supposed to be under the protection of the king, and so did not need weapons, but they took the precaution of building their houses with immensely

THE HIGH BRIDGE

(As it appeared in 1829)

thick walls, as you can see today in the Strait. But no walls, however thick, could protect them from the king himself. They were taxed unmercifully by Richard for his Crusades. John allowed them a breathing space for a few years, but in 1211 he turned against them and raised 66,000 marks by every imaginable cruelty. William the Marshall tried to protect them, but the people had been accustomed to persecuting them and the attacks continued. There were two violent attacks on the Jews' houses in Lincoln in 1219 and 1220, and a Jew and Jewess were murdered. The church joined in the persecution. Under the leadership of Stephen Langton, the church ordered that all Jews were to wear on their breasts a linen cloth two inches broad and four fingers long of a different colour from the rest of their clothes, so that Christians might be able to recognise and avoid them, and the Bishop of Lincoln, following the Archbishop's lead, tried to prevent them from having any dealings whatever with members of his diocese. So miserable was their condition made by 1254 that the Jews asked permission to leave the country. This was refused, but since no more money could be obtained from them, they were sold by the king to his brother, Richard, Earl of Cornwall, for £5,000.

Perhaps they might now have looked forward to better times, for Earl Richard was known to be a friend of the Jews, but in the following year the terrible story of Little St. Hugh began to be spread about, and from this time the Jews had no peace.

Little St. Hugh was a Lincoln boy of eight years of age who lived in the district at the bottom of Steep Hill, known as Dernstall, close to several Jewish houses. On an evening in August in 1255 he failed to return home, and it was learned that he had last been seen playing with Jewish children near the house of a Jew named Copin (sometimes written Jopin). According to one ballad that was sung

many years afterwards the Jew's daughter watched him playing ball
with his little friends :

> " He kept the ball there with his feet ;
> And catched it with his knee
> Till in at the cruel Jew's window
> With speed he garred it flee.
> Cast out the ball to me, fair maid,
> Cast out the ball to me.
> Ye ne'er shall have it, my bonny Sir Hugh,
> Till ye come up to me."

And when he went she lured him with an apple, red and white,
into an inner chamber, where, according to the legend, she murdered
him. At the end of ten days' search his body was found by his
mother in a well, and the Jews were at once accused of murdering
him. Terrified by the threats of torture and death the miserable
Copin declared that the child had been crucified by the Jews in
mockery of Christ's death and that when they tried to bury the body
"the earth vomited it forth," and so they placed it in the well.
From this time the child was regarded as a martyr. The canons
of the cathedral took possession of the body, and after exhibiting
it to crowds of pious sightseers, they buried it with all possible
honour. Copin had been promised his life if he confessed, but
the promise was broken. He was tied to a horse's tail and dragged
to the gallows on Canwick Hill and hanged. Ninety-one other
prominent Jews were arrested and sent to London, of whom eighteen
were hanged without trial of any kind. The rest were tried before
a jury of 24 knights and 24 London burgesses, and all but two were
condemned to death. A number of friars appealed to the king to
have mercy on them, but without success, and had it not been for
the intervention of the Earl of Cornwall this terrible sentence
would have been carried out.

The story of little St. Hugh is now discounted and has no foundation in
fact.

The story of little St. Hugh is only one of several stories that were told of the Jews by their enemies. How much truth there was in them it is impossible to say, but no sensible person can believe that the Jews of Lincoln had deliberately planned Hugh's murder. It is impossible to get at the truth because the Jews were never given a fair trial. Everybody *hoped* the Jews were guilty—the king, because he could confiscate their property ; the knights and burgesses, because many of them owed money to the Jews ; the people, because they were ignorant and superstituous ; and the church, because it could regard the child as a martyr and set up a shrine to his memory to which people would come with their offerings from far and wide. How could the Jews hope for justice with so many interests ranged against them ?

From this time the position of the Jews became worse than ever. The civil war between Henry III and the barons added to their difficulties. In 1266 a band of rebel barons, " The Disinherited " as they called themselves, who had been hiding in the Isle of Axholme, made a sudden attack on the city and took special care to burn the books of the Jews so that the records of debts owing to the Jews should be destroyed.

Another difficulty they had to face was that Christians were beginning to lend money at interest and the Jews were no longer necessary. In 1275 Edward I actually prohibited them from lending money at all ; this took away their chief means of livelihood. The Jews, of course, were unable to join a craft gild, or hold land, or go out to fight, because in order to do so they would have to take a Christian oath. Many of the Lincoln Jews now became more interested in the corn and woollen trades. A few, unable to earn their living in any other way, may have begun to clip the edges of coins, and in 1278 many Jews throughout the country were arrested and hanged on this charge, true or not. In London alone,

293 were executed. In 1290 Belasset de Wallingford, a Jewess who is said to have lived in the Jews' House in the Strait, was accused of this crime and hanged.

The end, however, was drawing near, for the king no longer needed the Jews, and so he could safely win the praise of the church by driving them out. Any Jew found in England after All Saints' Day 1290 was to be hanged, drawn and quartered. Sixteen thousand left England and though they were able to collect part of their debts before they left, their houses and remaining property were seized by the king. As we have seen, some of the property belonging to the Jews of Lincoln, instead of being handed over to the king, was kept back by the richer citizens, and a quarrel flared up which resulted in the city losing its privileges of self-government for ten years ; but the Jews, the innocent cause of all the trouble, had gone, and were not seen again in England for nearly four hundred years.

CHAPTER IX.

LINCOLN AND THE WOOL TRADE.

During the fourteenth century great changes took place in Lincoln. It had lost its privileged position as the only centre of foreign trade in the county and its rich colony of Jews had been dispersed, but it was still a very lively and prosperous city. In 1291 it had been chosen by Edward I as a staple town and all the merchants, whether English or foreign, who wished to export wool, hides or leather from the counties of Lincolnshire, Nottinghamshire, Derbyshire, Leicestershire and Northamptonshire, had to come to Lincoln to do their trading. Only in this way, it was thought, could the king be sure of collecting his dues on the goods that went out of the country.

From all parts of the Midland Counties the wool was brought—by road and river, on the backs of men and horses and mules, to the warehouses and wharves that stood near Stamp End. The abbot of Kirkstead had his own wharf on the Witham below Sheepwash Grange ; and in Wigford, where much of the trade was done, stood massive stone houses, belonging to wool merchants and nobles. As the wool was brought it was weighed by an officer of the king on the royal "steelyard" or weighing machine, and when the tax was paid it was sealed by the king's officer, and could then be sent abroad.

The staple had its own staff of officers, at the head of which was a mayor elected by the merchants of the staple, and it had also a special court consisting half of foreigners and half of Englishmen in order to see that justice was done between buyer and seller, and that neither foreigner nor Englishman broke the rules.

But the chief difficulty was to prevent wool being smuggled out of England without paying toll. The rich Florentines who lived in the city were continually accused of this. Load after load, it was said, had been shipped down the Witham without paying toll, and the neighbouring Cistercian abbeys, as we have seen (see p. 73) had to be warned by the king himself, even before the staple had been set up at Lincoln, against allowing their monks to buy up small parcels of wool and export them abroad without sending them to Lincoln. And there were other causes of dispute. The Abbot of Kirkstead quarrelled with the city over his claim to have the wharf of Sheepwash Grange all to himself, and when the notorious local baron, William de Kyme, seized Dockdyke Haven into his own hands and levied toll on all ships that passed, there was nothing for it but to call in the king's bailiff to keep him in order.

These were the great days of Lincoln's history. Her streets hummed with life. Strange tongues drawn from the Mediterranean and the Baltic mingled with the broad accents of Lincolnshire and the Midlands. Men of the Derbyshire Dales and the Lincolnshire Wolds, of the Trent valley and the Fens, of Sherwood and Charnwood, bought and sold, laughed, prayed and wrangled with the men of Florence, Lubeck and Danzig. Monks vied with merchants in avoiding tolls, and abbots, no less than knights, struggled for special privileges.

Lincoln, in common with the rest of the country, suffered terribly from the Black Death, which reached the city in 1349. We have no account of the local effects of the plague written at the time simply as the record of the epidemic, but we have records made for other purposes, which enable us to see what happened. The records of clergymen appointed to parishes show that a great many of the city clergy died, and the rolls of the city court, or Burgmanmot, show that the number of wills dealt with by the court rose from an average of under five in a normal year to 105 in 1349. Of course these wills were made by members of the richer classes only. The poorer people made no will, but probably suffered more heavily than the richer citizens. The plague began in April, and ended suddenly in August. Probate of wills became the main business of the city court. Wills dealing with the same property were proved twice in a single day ! It has been estimated that over half of the population of Lincoln perished in the Black Death, the mayor being among the victims. For a few years after the pestilence the city made rapid strides towards recovery, but other towns were growing up and casting jealous eyes on Lincoln's privileges. In 1369 the blow fell ; the staple was removed to Boston and Lincoln was robbed of its last privilege.

From this time onwards we hear nothing but dismal stories of decay and growing poverty. Whereas, in the time of the staple there used to be ten or twelve great merchants of Calais in the town to buy up the wool, there were only three in King Richard II's reign. Lords and gentlemen no longer came near, and craftsmen and victuallers had departed to more prosperous places, so that the streets where they had dwelt were void and their houses down. Many men who had been apprenticed in the city had to go elsewhere to find work and no new craftsmen or travellers came to dwell there.

We should remember that this tale of woe was told in the hopes of obtaining a reduction of taxation, and perhaps it makes things appear worse than they really were. At any rate there were still many traders and craftsmen at Lincoln, and the gilds, in which the craftsmen were organised, continued to flourish for centuries after this.

CHAPTER X.

THE GILDS.

We have so far confined ourselves to the merchants and traders organised in the merchant gild and the staple, but besides them there were many varieties of workmen—weavers, who wove the wool which their wives had spun ; fullers, who "fulled" the cloth, *i.e.*, felted it ; shearmen, who clipped it ; dyers, who dyed it. Then there were smiths of all kinds to make horseshoes, bridles, buckles, helmets, swords and suits of armour ; carpenters, joiners, masons, shoemakers and leather workers of all kinds. There were also the boatmen on the river and the fishermen of the pools. There would be the taverners who kept the taverns, and alewives who sold ale to passers-by in dingy little wayside shops. There were the provision merchants—victuallers, as they were called—who kept the city supplied with food, carters from the big manor houses bringing in supplies of meat and flour to the market, and porters carrying bales of cloth from the quayside near the High Bridge. Besides all these, there were the workmen connected with the religious houses, the castle and the cathedral ; lay brethren, who worked in the fields and the gardens of the monasteries ; soldiers on guard in the castle walls and servitors in the hall ; and at the cathedral there were the masons and stonecutters who were still at work on their scaffolding, putting the finishing touches to the roof and towers ; and there were also other kinds of workmen, the artists patiently sitting over their illuminated manuscripts and missals, like those which you may still see in the cathedral library.

And just as the merchants had their merchant gild, so did the different groups of workmen have their craft gilds. As early as the reign of Henry II there were 200 weavers in Lincoln whose gild paid £6 a year to the town's farm, and in the course of the next fifty years others appeared. They had important and useful duties to perform, such as the fixing of hours of work, wages and prices. For instance, the barbers' gild in 1440 fixed the price of a shave as follows : for a poor person, ¼d. ; for a priest, ½d. Perhaps the priest had to pay more because of his tonsure. They were specially anxious to prevent anyone holding up supplies in order to increase the price. This was called "forestalling" or "regrating," and was regarded in those days as a sort of robbery of the community, the worst of crimes. They took care of the sick and old among their members who could no longer work, and orphan children were taken into the homes of the members and trained in the craft of the gild. They also had religious and educational duties ; they buried the poorer members who could not afford a funeral, and paid a priest to say prayers for their souls. Each gild had its patron saint, whom it commemorated in solemn procession with a huge candle at the head, and many gilds had their own chantries in the cathedral or the parish churches and their own chantry priests. The chantry priest was frequently a schoolmaster also, and he could sometimes chose the brighter boys in the gild and train them for the cathedral school, or even the university. Thus the gilds took the place, to some extent, of the elementary and secondary schools of today. They also insisted upon a technical training through the system of apprenticeship. The gilds touched the lives of their members on all sides, on the material side of wages and hours and conditions of work, and on the side of religion and culture and the every day joys and sorrows that are the lot of men and women throughout history. It would be very interesting and valuable to have the history of each of the leading craft gilds in Lincoln, but unfortunately very little is known of some of them.

THE WEAVERS' GILD.

The first and perhaps the most important of all the craft gilds in Lincoln was the weavers' gild, which was already organised in 1157, and in course of time it was followed by gilds of fullers and dyers. At this time Lincoln became especially well known for its red cloth and, perhaps, for the so-called Lincoln green that is supposed to have been worn by Robin Hood's men. The cloth was made in the homes of the workmen or in small workshops. Some cloth was also made in the villages around and brought to the cloth market for sale. As early as 1182 the sheriff was buying cloth in Lincolnshire for the king's needs—an ell of scarlet 6s. 8d. ; an ell of blanket 3s. Some of the city workmen wished to go outside into the villages nearby to work at their trade. This was forbidden by the city counsel, no doubt because it was feared that workers in the country, who would not be controlled by the gild, might employ cheap country labour and so spoil the market for the craftsmen in the city, and the fullers and dyers were not allowed to full or dye any cloth that had not been made in the city, even for their own use. Thus the craftsmen in the city had a monopoly of finished cloth. From this we can conclude that the weavers had some good friends in authority, and that the fullers and dyers were not so lucky ! At any rate, we know that the fullers and dyers were not freemen of the city, while the members of all the other gilds were. At this time many clever foreign craftsmen from Flanders were coming to England, especially to Norwich and Norfolk, and they brought new methods of working fine cloth. Few, if any of them, came to Lincoln. Was it because of these restrictions ? At any rate the cloth trade in Lincoln declined, while in Norfolk and other districts it flourished. Whereas in the time of Henry II there were said to be 200 weavers in Lincoln, in 1321 there were none. Apparently there was some revival in 1348, for in that year we hear of "many Lincoln citizens who kept hired weavers making cloth for sale," but the damage was done, and the Lincoln cloth industry never regained its prosperity. Time after time the city council, and also the magistrates in the county, tried to bring back prosperity to the cloth industry, and in 1784 a factory was established in Lincoln to make woollen cloths called "stuffs," and in order to give it encouragement an annual Stuff Ball was started, which was held in all but about fifteen exceptional years until about 1930. Although the manufacture of cloth had long since ceased, it was revived in 1938, but given up again during the war which began in 1939. The first ball took place on the 17th November, 1785, at Alford, and free admission was given to all ladies who would wear orange coloured stuff gowns and petticoats, spun and woven in Lincolnshire, those who had spun their own gowns to wear white ribbons, others blue ; and to all gentlemen who would appear without any cotton or silk in their dress except stockings. The colours for the ladies' dresses were changed every year to make sure that they would have new ones ! But the " Stuff " factory did not prosper. It was closed down and eventually turned into dwelling houses.

THE LATER GILDS.

Although the days of Lincoln's prosperity had passed after the staple was removed, there were still several industries sufficiently important to have craft gilds. The tanners, the cordwainers, the barber surgeons, the glovers, the smiths, the tailors, the tilers, and the carpenters, all had gilds in the reign of Elizabeth. Each of these gilds included workers in related trades ; for instance, the glovers included all other kinds of leather workers, the girdlers, skinners, pinners, pointers, scriveners and parchment makers. The gild of the smiths included ironmongers, armourers, spurriers, cutlers, horse marshals and wire drawers. There was one gild for tilers, masons, bricklayers, plasterers, pavers, tilemakers, glasiers, lime makers, milners (millwrights) and thekers (thatchers). Why did these different kinds of workmen join in one gild ? Possibly because they were trying to prevent competition amongst themselves, and so agreed to join one gild in order to settle their difficulties.

This kind of thing was happening in all the towns of England in the sixteenth and seventeenth centuries. By the eighteenth century the separate gilds had usually joined together to keep out "foreigners," that is, tradesmen and workers from other towns—and were busy prosecuting them before the magistrates for setting up a trade in their town without being apprenticed. But trade was good and there were many rich masters wanting men in the eighteenth century, and also new machines, which could be worked by unskilled labour, and even by children, were coming into use. Consequently it was impossible to insist upon apprenticeship any longer except in the most highly skilled trades. Labour became "free"—that is, the employer bought it as cheaply as possible, as he would any other commodity. The gilds, which were organ-

Stone figure at the Cathedral representing a Pilgrim

isations of masters as well as of men, slowly broke down. Most of them vanished between 1660 and 1700.

THE RELIGIOUS SIDE OF THE GILDS.

You will notice that the gilds became more and more concerned with social and economic questions and less and less with religion. We hear no more of solemn processions with lighted candles to the cathedral, of speeding their brethren to the Holy Land on a pilgrimage,—of plays and masques and celebrations on holy days, but only of apprenticeship regulations, wage contracts and hours of labour. In the middle ages the gilds had organised the religion, the education and also the entertainment of their members. The gild was a social club plus an insurance society, plus a trade union, plus a kind of Rotary club of masters. Some gilds existed for nothing but religious and social purposes. There were the gilds of St. Benedict, of St. Anne, Corpus Christi, and especially the great gild of St. Mary. We hear of them especially after the Black Death, possibly because people had been so terrified that for a time, at any rate, they became more pious.

They had many interesting practices. If one of the brethren of the gild of St. Anne, in the parish of St. Peter at the Skinmarket, went on a pilgrimage to Rome or the Holy Land, the whole gild walked in procession with him to the Cross on Lincoln Green. The graceman, that is the master of the gild, after blessing him, gave him 2d. The wardens gave him a penny each, and every gild member a halfpenny. On his return he was met at the same place and conducted with joy and honour to the cathedral, and then home.

As time went on we see another side of the work of the religious gilds. The processions which they organised in honour of their patron saints gradually took the form of religious plays, which all the citizens of Lincoln, men and women alike, were expected to support. The subscription was 4d. for man and wife, and the money was spent on organising a magnificent procession on St. Anne's Day, or the Sunday following, in which all the gilds of the city took part. Each gild brought out its "pageant," a kind of theatre on wheels consisting of two stages. The lower part was fitted with curtains and was used as a dressing room. The upper part was the stage on which the play was produced. Each gild tried to find the kind of play for which it was most suited. The shipbuilders would choose a play like " Noah's Ark," for instance. Plays enacted at Lincoln represented the lives of St. James, St. Clare and King Robert of Sicily. Another favourite play was the story of Tobias, and in order to present it the players had to have the following pieces of scenery : the City of Jerusalem, the City of Nineveh, a firmament with a fiery cloud, a double cloud and a model of Hell Mouth ! The great procession with the "pageants" of all the gilds started from High Bridge and went to the cathedral. It was one of the greatest events in the year's happenings. The aldermen sent their servants with lighted torches to join the procession, and ladies and gentlemen of the county lent their rich costumes to the leading players, and sightseers from all the countryside poured into the city to watch it pass. But sometimes there was a plague in the city, and there was danger in lending costumes or in coming to watch, and then it fell to the aldermen, sheriffs and chamberlains to provide costumes.

But if the corporation helped in the procession, it also shared in the profits, and when Henry VIII, in 1545, threatened to dissolve the gilds and take their property, the corporation of Lincoln made haste to force the richest of the Lincoln gilds, the great gild of St. Mary, to give up its property to the city. They confiscated the funds of the gild and all its plate and jewellery, to the value of £24 13s. 4d., which would be equal to much more today. The gild of St. Anne followed, and all the ornaments, plate and jewellery, which it kept for use in the procession, were ordered to be sold for the benefit of the corporation.

In spite of this the procession continued for a further twenty years. Possibly the order was not carried out, or perhaps the corporation took over the property of the gild in order to keep it from being confiscated by the king.

Another very interesting work of the religious gilds was to lend out the money of the gild to its members who wished to set up in trade, and to share the profits with the gild. For instance, the gild of St. Benedict ordered the brothers and sisters to come to a meeting, which they called a "mornspeech", in the church on the Sunday after the feast of St. Michael, and those who had borrowed money from the gild were to bring with them half the profits they had made. Thus the gild acted as a kind of banker to its members.

But perhaps the chief reason for the popularity of the religious gilds, especially in time of plague or war, was that they provided against sickness and funeral expenses for their members, and employed a priest to say masses for their souls when they died. We should remember that everybody believed at that time in the doctrine of Purgatory, and thought that the offering up of prayers for the dead would cause their souls to go to Heaven more quickly. The poorer citizens, who could not pay for the prayers themselves, were able to obtain the services of the chantry priest by joining the gild.

The richest of all the gilds was the great gild of St. Mary. It had two chaplains who celebrated daily in the church of St. Andrew in Wigford for the good of the brothers and sisters of the departed members. It was in existence during the reign of Henry III, for he was a member, and it used for its hall a very fine old building which may still be seen, and is called " John of Gaunt's Stables." The hall was originally built about 1160.   If you look at it you will see a band of ornament very elaborately carved.   The gild of St.

The Norman House in the Courtyard of St. Mary's Guildhall

Mary, to whom it belonged, must have been very rich to uphold such a magnificent hall, but where trade and industry are flourishing, it is only to be expected that religious organisations will be numerous and rich, and this, as we have seen, was the case with Lincoln in the middle ages.

ST. MARY'S GUILDHALL

(Popularly known as John O'Gaunt's Stables)

CHAPTER XI.

MARKETS AND FAIRS.

This long account of trade and industry in medieval Lincoln leaves one important question unanswered. How were the goods distributed? How did buyer and seller come into contact at a time when shops as we know them did not exist? The answer is, by means of markets and fairs held at regular intervals at certain recognised places. They probably originated in religious assemblies of pious worshippers who had come from far and near to make their offerings at some famous shrine. Here would be a brisk demand for candles for the processions, for robes, and girdles—and for board and lodging for strangers. It was also possible to exchange goods with the strangers themselves, for pilgrims were sometimes merchants as well. Here also would be the "peace" of the church, and later of the king himself, to protect the merchants in their dangerous calling, and safeguard the sanctity of contracts solemnly entered into under the shadow of the market cross.

For this protection merchants had to pay, of course, and the "owner" of the market or fair exacted heavy tolls on everything that was bought or sold. Quarrels frequently arose regarding the amount of tolls, and owing to a quarrel at Lincoln in 1361 on this question we learn that the market tolls were as follows :—

For every horse bought or sold	1d.
For every ox	$\frac{1}{2}$d.
For every cart	2d.
For a ship	4d.
For 24 two-year-old sheep	1d.
For every quarter of corn	1d.

But among the persons interested in the question of tolls was the king. No fair or market could be held without an express grant from him, and in return he expected to be paid for this valuable privilege. Lincoln received many such grants. In Edward III's time markets were held on Mondays, Wednesdays and Fridays, and on these days the streets were thronged with booths and stalls set up by local craftsmen, country traders and farmers for the exchange of their wares. From a very early time the traders in the same articles tended to set up their stalls together in the same place, and so different areas came to be allotted for the sale of the different kinds of produce—meat, fish, pots, corn, leather, butter, cloth, skins—that were brought to the market. Though the sites of the markets were occasionally altered, we can still identify a considerable number of them ; for instance, the corn market (which boasted of a market cross) was held on the Steep Hill from the Jews' House upwards. Later it was moved to the Cornhill. The meat market was formerly in Upper High Street, but moved in 1774 to the Shambles in Clasketgate. There was a slaughter house here too, much frequented in the nineteenth century by the children of the neighbourhood, to whom the finer points of pole-axing a lively steer were matters of great moment. Another market was the Peltry on the east side of High Street just above the Stonebow, where skins were sold. Cloth was sold on a site between Steep Hill and Michaelgate, which is still called " The Drapery." The butter market was held in Newland, but the " Butter Cross " is supposed to have been pulled down at the Reformation as a "Monument of Superstition." The market was transferred to the High Street, above the Stonebow, and in 1736 the " Butter Market," which served until 1937, was erected to shelter the stall holders. But besides these—and other marketing centres—High Street itself was blocked with stalls on market days from St. Mark's to the High

Bridge, and it was not until the Lincoln Corn Exchange and Markets Company was formed in 1847 that other accommodation was found.

But there were two periods of the year which stood out above all others in those days of Lincoln's medieval greatness. These were the periods of the fairs—the Great Fairs of St. Botolph in June and July and of St. Hugh in November. To these fairs merchants came from all parts of England, and many parts of Europe too.

At what period the fair of St. Botolph originated we do not know, but in 1327 Edward III, after an enquiry to see that no injustice was being done to anyone else, confirmed the right of the city to hold a fair from the feast of St. Botolph (17th June) to that of St. Peter and Paul (29th June), and extended the period of the fair for a further thirteen days until July 12th, making a total of 25 days ! During this hectic twenty-five days the life of the city was completely transformed. Here every variety of native produce could be bought ; wool, of course, from the surrounding shires, tin from Cornwall, salt from the Worcestershire springs, lead from Derbyshire, iron from Sussex. Here the bailiff purchased his farm implements and stores of salt and sheep medicines, the nobleman bought his armour and war horse, the lady her robes and dresses. There were costly spices of the East, and silks and velvets from the looms of Italy and France. The Spaniard brought his wonderful steel blades, the Norwegian his tar, the Gascon his wine, and the Swede his furs and amber.

Nowadays we can spend our money as fast as we get it—sometimes faster—but in those days the opportunities for spending were far fewer, and when the fair came round there was an orgy of buying and selling for which people had been saving up for months. Enormous amounts of money (for those days) must have changed hands and the tolls which the city charged were an important part of its revenue.

But the city had no direct authority over the fairs, and in order to see that justice was done between buyer and seller, native and stranger, it was necessary to set up a special court for the period of the fair. This was the court of " Pie Powder"—originally " Pieds poudrés"—which means dusty feet, the feet of people that have come from afar, who had to get their cases settled immediately so that they could go on to the next fair without waiting for the meeting of the local court. It sat every day during the period of the fair, and dealt with cases with the least possible delay. The president of the court was the chief officer of the borough, and with him sat a number of assessors drawn from the merchants themselves, half of them being aliens when the case concerned a foreign merchant. The law which they administered was drawn from the practices of merchants all over Europe, and was more modern in many ways than that of the local court. It was, in fact, a kind of international law recognised by merchants everywhere. A court of this kind existed in Lincoln in the reign of Richard III but there are no records of its transactions.

Besides St. Botolph's, there was also a fair, as we have read, at the feast of St. Hugh (17th November). It was granted by Henry IV in 1409 and was held on " The Croft" until 1803, when it was transferred to Broadgate. St. Hugh's Croft was on the south side of Monks Road, where Croft Street and St. Hugh's Street now stand. Originally the fair lasted thirty days from 17th November, and all kinds of merchandise were brought for sale, though in later years St. Hugh's Croft was used for the sale of cattle, sheep and, horses, and other merchandise was disposed of in " The Friars," i.e., the grounds of the Grey Friars' house. Later still (1707) the section of the fair held at the Friars was moved to High Street, and the Enclosure Act of 1803 authorised the transfer of the horse, cattle and sheep fair to Broadgate, where it was to be held on 28th

November. When the calendar was altered in 1757, eleven days were omitted, which accounts for the fair commencing on 28th November instead of the 17th.

Two other fairs were granted at a later date, one by Charles II, commencing on the second Tuesday in April and lasting four days, and the other by William III on the first Wednesday in September and lasting three days. The first included a horse fair which was one of the most important in England. For the first two days it was held in the High Street, which was lined with horses, from the Bow to St. Mary le Wigford's church, and on the third it was transferred to Broadgate, and it remained until recent years a most important event. As the time for the April fair drew near an air of expectancy stirred in the old town, just waking from its winter sleep. Houses were repainted and the fronts were washed and dashed. Foreigners and blackguards of all complexions, we are told, dropped in to prey upon the unwary. There was chaffering for horses in inn yards, and a medley of tongues from all over England as the fine Lincolnshire horses were put through their paces. But with the coming of the motor car the fair declined, and the tractor has almost killed it. In 1929 it bade farewell to the city streets and was moved to the West Common, but it is now a faint shadow of its former self.

The same sad story may be told of the April sheep fair. Once one of the most important fairs in England—and one of the most wonderful sights anywhere—at which 70,000 sheep were bought and sold, the sheep fair has dwindled to insignificance. The regular weekly market and the ease of transport have taken away its importance, but in its heyday a century ago, it ranked with the horse fair as one of the bright spots in Lincoln's year. It was formerly held on the Old Sheep Square, now occupied by St. Swithin's Church. In 1846 it was moved to the Vine Closes, above Monks' Road, and in 1878 it was transferred to the West Common, where it is still held.

The Horse Fair ceased in 1952.
The Sheep Fair ceased c.1941.

The modern April fair is a survival of the fair granted by Charles II, but amusement has largely replaced business. The pleasures of the people who attended the fairs were always provided for by enterprising showmen and traders. In earlier days the mechanical music and roundabouts were absent, but bazaars, menageries, circuses, marionettes, monstrosities, ghost shows, boxing booths and peep shows supplied plenty of opportunities for spending money. In the middle of the nineteenth century these attractions were to be found on a piece of land between Newland and West Parade, now partly occupied by St. Martin's Church. About 1872, when the old fair ground was being used for building, the pleasure fair was moved to the Cheviot Close near the Arboretum, and soon afterwards to the land between the Sessions House and cattle market. In 1943 it was moved to the South Common.

St. Martin's Church was demolished in 1970.

CHAPTER XII.

THE RELIGIOUS HOUSES OF LINCOLN.

We have now seen how Lincoln was governed in the Middle Ages. We have seen the city at the height of her prosperity as a staple town, and the centre of the trade of all the neighbouring counties, and we have seen how the people, both rich and poor, organised themselves into gilds and fraternities to make their lives happier in this world and to prepare their souls for the next.

Monks' Abbey

But there was one group of men and women, who, in theory at least, stood outside all these activities, who were not supposed to take part in industry or trade, and were not members of any gilds. These were the monks and friars, who lived in the numerous religious houses that existed in Lincoln at this time.

Here is a list of them all, together with the approximate date at which they were founded, and the places, as far as we know them, in which they stood :—

Monks	Cell of St. Mary's Abbey, York	Monks' Abbey	Before 1275
Canons	St. Catherine's Priory	West of High Street opposite South Common	c. 1148
Friars	Augustinian (Eremite) Carmelite (White) Dominican (Black) Franciscan (Grey) of the Sack	Newport L.M.S. Railway Station Sessions House The Museum North bank of Witham near Thornbridge	c. 1270 c. 1269 Before 1238 c. 1230 Before 1266
Hospitals	Holy Innocents Holy Sepulchre St. Bartholomew St. Giles St. Leonard St. Mary	South Common Adjoining St. Catherine's West of the Castle Wragby Road West of Castle Unknown	Before 1135 c. 1123 Before 1314 Before 1280 Before 1300 Before 1311

MONKS' ABBEY.

You will see from this list that Lincoln was well provided with religious houses. St. Mary Magdalene's Cell, or Monks' Abbey as it is called, belonged to the Abbey of St. Mary at York, which was given land here in the time of William the Conqueror. The monks of St. Mary belonged to the Benedictine order and were known as the Black Monks because they wore a tunic, cowl and hood of black material. The cell of Monks' Abbey was small and had only a prior and two or three monks, and sometimes no monks at all.

A city like Lincoln, busy and humming with life, could hardly have been a suitable place for monks. They were supposed to devote the whole of their lives to prayer and religious duties and not to undertake any business in the outside world. That is why they are called "regular" clergy as distinct from the *seculars*, who conducted services in the parish churches and served their cures in other ways. In consequence the monks were not very popular in the town. They no doubt relieved the poor who came to beg at their gate, but they were not supposed to go out, as the friars did, to seek for those who needed help.

The prior and the monks who occupied the cell were mainly concerned in collecting the rents of the lands which had at various times been allotted to it, and as far as we know, took no part in the life of the city. It was dissolved, along with the other religious houses, by Henry VIII, and the lands which were valued at £23 6s. 3d. were taken into the king's hands. The city had tried very hard to obtain them, but all of them were granted to two merchants (possibly because they could afford to pay more). At a later date the Monks' Leys became a common belonging to the freemen. The buildings served for a time as farm buildings, but were eventually allowed to fall into ruin.

Three walls of the chapel form the chief remains. The tracery of the windows is in the early perpendicular style, which indicates that the chapel was built in the late fourteenth or early fifteenth century. At the western end of the south wall is a pillar which stood

A Stone Head on
the Cathedral

at the corner of a transept running southwards from this point. To the west of the chapel one wall of the domestic buildings still stands, containing a doorway and the remains of a window which once lighted a room about 18 feet long by 16 feet broad.

On the north-east side of the buildings the low ground, now used as a playground, marks the position of the mill-pond, which may have supplied the monks with fish.

Just to the east of the church, on the river side of the old mill-pond, are the remains of a stone building which probably contained the water-wheel for grinding corn. A ring in the Usher Gallery is said to have belonged to the prior of the cell.

The ruins and grounds were given to the city by The Hon. W. F. Massey-Mainwaring.

ST. CATHERINE'S PRIORY.

Perhaps the most interesting and important of the religious houses was the Gilbertine Priory of St. Catherine. It stood just outside the walls between High Street and the Witham, and was founded about 1148 for canons, that is, religious men who lived together in a community, but who also acted as parish priests in the parishes belonging to the house. Lay sisters, or religious women, who had not taken the vows of a nun, were soon introduced to look after the sick and the children in the hospital of St. Sepulchre, which was attached to the Priory.

It was here that Queen Eleanor's body was prepared for burial in 1290, and the first of the famous Eleanor Crosses was erected just outside the Priory on Swine Green. A stone, which is said to be part of one of the statues of Eleanor which were on the Cross, is now kept in the entrance to the castle. Eleanor had died at Harby, a few miles west of Lincoln. Some parts of her body were buried in the cathedral, where there is a reproduction of the monument which was placed over them.

St. Catherine's Priory had land in many parts of Lincolnshire and Nottinghamshire, and its sales of wool in the early fourteenth century averaged 35 sacks a year, and each sack weighed 26 stones. The price varied from 10 to 22½ marks a sack, according to quality, which would amount to about £250 to £500 a year. Yet in 1332 the house was in debt to Italian moneylenders and merchants to the amount of £956, a very large sum for those days. At first sight this looks like bad management, but most of the debt was not due to trading losses. The prior had been appointed by the king to collect a tax from the clergy near Lincoln. In order to pay for his war with Scotland Edward III had borrowed money from merchants of Florence and Genoa and instructed the prior to repay the debt out of the money collected by the prior from the clergy.

The house had many expenses and was involved in costly quarrels. The king expected the prior to find hospitality for his friends when they required it. One of them was Christiana de Hauville, who came to live in the Priory by order of Edward II, after she had lost her husband and three sons and all her property in the Scotch wars. The prior had to find horses and carts for the king's campaigns, and he was supposed to keep in repair the churches which, at various times, had been allotted to him. The expense of hospitality was heavy, especially as the house stood near the city gate and made a convenient halting place for distinguished travellers while the city prepared to welcome them. It was from here that the bishops walked barefoot on their way to the cathedral to be enthroned, the cloth on which they walked being afterwards given to the poor.

More than one king made his last halt here before entering the city, and judges of Assize reined up here for refreshment long after it ceased to be a Priory.

But the prior had other more serious trouble. The Duke of Lancaster seized some of his lands, and in 1323 a violent quarrel flared up with the abbot of Kirkstead. The abbot's monks, it was said, had seized four of the prior's ships at Timberland Ferry, and ten nets from his fishery, while the abbot in his turn complained that the prior's men had poached the abbot's fisheries and trampled down his corn at Canwick. The city of Lincoln complained that the prior had encroached upon the city's land in some of his building. But the worst period for the Priory came after the Black Death. Its lands were no longer so valuable because there were fewer tenants to work them. Labour was scarce, wages high, and taxation was heavy, and soon the house was again in debt. The prior had to economise at the expense of the parishes which belonged to the house. For instance, he neglected to appoint a chaplain to Saxby Church while continuing to draw the tithes, and though he was compelled to add to the stipend of the vicar of Alford, he managed (with the help of the pope) to avoid appointing vicars to Newark and Mere, but sent canons, whom he could recall at any time. The most famous prior was Robert Holgate, a type of Churchman—and there were many at this time—who was willing to win promotion and riches at the expense of his order. In 1529 he went to London, and took with him, it was said, a gold cup and two censers belonging to the house. He became chaplain to Thomas Cromwell, who made him Master of the whole order of Gilbertine houses, although it was known that he intended to dissolve them, and William Griffiths became Prior of St. Catherine's. In 1538 the house at Lincoln was the first to surrender and in 1545, in return for Holgate's valuable services, the king made him Archbishop of York.

The house had probably been getting poorer and weaker for many years before it was actually dissolved. It paid a Lincolnshire landowner, Lord Hussey of Sleaford, to act as agent or steward for its property (he was doing this for twenty other houses at the same time) and its revenues at the dissolution were just over £200 a year, whereas in 1254 they were estimated at £270 a year, besides the trade in wool. When the house was dissolved, the prior was given a pension of £40 a year, and the canons from 40 shillings to £5 6s. 8d. a year each, but five lay sisters, who refused to agree to the surrender, got nothing. It should be remembered that the salary of a parish priest at that time was about £7 a year.

After the dissolution the house was known as St. Catherine's Hall and was used as a residence by its various owners and as a place of entertainment for distinguished guests. On one occasion King James I stayed there, and among the guests was a young man, John Hutchinson, who later signed the death warrant of James' son Charles. In the eighteenth century the building was allowed to fall into ruin and was pulled down, and now the only reminder we have of it is the name, St. Catherine's, by which the district in which it stood is known today.

THE FRIARS.

It was not until 1230 that the first friary was founded in Lincoln. By that time the monks had been there for nearly 200 years, while the parish clergy had been there for longer still. Why should the friars come? Were there not enough churchmen in Lincoln, with its cathedral and its staff of priests, its many parish churches, a priory, a monastic cell, numerous hospitals, and no one knows how many chantry priests attached to the gilds? We may say quite safely that out of every five adults, one belonged, in some capacity, to the church. And then came the friars.

Strange as it may seem, the friars were very welcome wherever they went. Unlike the monks they mixed with the common people. They built their houses in their midst. They sought out the poor and sick, and shared whatever they had. They built their large churches and called everyone in to pray and sing with them and to listen to their sermons. Unlike the parish priests, they loved to preach, and after their services they gave the sacraments, just as the parish priests did. The priests were furious. There was war between them and the friars as there used to be between Anglicans and Nonconformists. But the friars continued and their friaries grew and prospered —indeed they prospered too well, as we shall see. The priests took their revenge by saying that the friars were foxes and the people who listened to them geese. From the picture above it looks as though the dean and chapter of the cathedral shared this view, as they allowed this carving to be placed in the choir stalls.

Wood carving in the cathedral of fox preaching to geese

THE FRANCISCANS.

The first of the friars to come to Lincoln were the Franciscans known as the Grey Friars, or Friars Minor. They were sworn to utter poverty and to live upon the gifts which were made to them in return for their services. They came to Lincoln about 1230 and were given a piece of land and a home by the citizens near the hall of the merchants' gild. They prospered rapidly and in 1237 the hall itself was handed over to them and, by 1300, their numbers grew to fifty-three. Their property eventually occupied about four acres and extended from Silver Street on the north to Saltergate on the south, and from Free School Lane on the west to the city wall along Broadgate on the east. They were frequently accused of encroaching on the city wall itself and so injuring the defences. There were quarrels also with the parish priests who tried to prevent their parishioners from going to the friars to confess, but the bishops generally supported the friars and continued to give them licences to hear confessions in spite of the protests of the parish priests. The

St. Mary's Conduit

friars were also on good terms with the city fathers, who gave them stone from demolished churches with which to repair their house, and permitted them to lay water pipes or a conduit in the public highway wherever it was most convenient. The pipes ran from a spring on the hillside east of the city and carried a supply of fresh water to the house. When the convent was dissolved by Henry VIII their valuable water supply was handed over to the city by the king, and pipes were laid to three new " Castles of the Conduit," of which one may be seen today at St. Mary le Wigford's Church.

The house itself continued to be used for many different purposes. In 1567 a school was established here, which continued to be carried on in the same building until 1900. But only the upper rooms were required for this purpose. The lower rooms were used at various times to store gun powder, as a house of correction, as a school for spinning, or a Jersey School (so named because of the Jersey spinning wheel which was used by the inmates), and then from 1833 to 1862 as a Mechanics' Institute, Library and Reading Room. In 1907 the building became the Museum which we see today. The

The House of the Grey Friars

THE CATHEDRAL AND OLD ST. PAUL'S CHURCH
(From a drawing dated 1784, by S. R. Grimm)

style of the archcitecture of the Museum indicates that it was one of the early buildings of the friars. At first it had only one floor, but before long it was divided into upper and lower rooms. The floor of the upper room, supported by the pillars and vaulting of the room below, cuts across the original windows. The fire place and chimney on the north side of the upper room were obviously added after the new floor was made. The upper room was used as the chapel of the friary. A recess with two bowls and a water drain, which was used at communion services, still remains in the south wall near the east end of the room. The undivided building was lighted at first by single lancet windows, some of which, now blocked up, can still be traced. The sills of the windows on the south side were higher than those on the north side, probably because the cloisters were built close up to the church on the south side. The three-light window in the east end probably dates from about 1260. Above it is an early "fish" shaped window. The other windows are imitations of Tudor windows which were inserted during the nineteenth century.

THE DOMINICANS.

The next most important order of friars to come to Lincoln was called the Dominicans or Black Friars. Their house stood between Lindum Road and Monks' Road. It is said that Rosemary Lane takes its name from the apothecary's garden belonging to it. They came before 1238, and by 1300 there were 47 of them in the friary. They busied themselves, among other things, in making a road from their house in Lincoln as far as the road leading to Greetwell (Monks' Road) and in laying pipes, or a "conduit" as it was called, to carry water from a spring on land belonging to 'Monks Abbey' along the highway to their house. They also tried to help some of the Jews accused of the murder of St. Hugh, and they became so popular during the next century that many gifts of

houses and lands were bestowed on them.   Though they had made
a solemn vow of poverty, they became the owners of a considerable
amount of property, and the land on which their house stood occupied
ten acres.   Like all the other religious houses it was dissolved by
Henry VIII, and passed into the hands of the same two men who
bought so much monastic property, John Broxholme and John Bellow.

THE WHITE FRIARS.

The " White Friars," or Carmelites, had a house here too, of
thirty or forty members.   It stood on the west side of High Street
where the L.M. and S. Railway Station now stands, and must have
been an important one since the king himself lodged here for a time,
and it was in the great hall of the White Friars that the parliament
which he called at Lincoln in 1316 assembled.   It had a good
library too, which was unusual, most of the other religious houses
in Lincoln having no more than two or three books at the time of
the dissolution.

THE FRIARS OF THE SACK.

A fourth house of friars has to be mentioned.   Its occupants
were known by the curious name of the " Friars of the Sack," on
account of their coarse dress, though their full title was " The
Friars of the Penance of Jesus Christ."

They came before 1266, and their house was situated on the
north side of the Witham near Thornbridge, but by 1300 only four
of them remained in the house, and by 1307 it was empty.   As the
house stood near the Witham it occupied a valuable commercial
site and the monks of Barlings Abbey tried to get possession of it
in order to set up a warehouse in which to store their tanned hides,
wool, corn and other produce, until they could sell them at a profit,
but they were not allowed to do so, lest it should injure the trade
of the city.

L.M. and S. Railway Station is now St. Marks Station.

THE AUGUSTINIAN FRIARS.

There was another house, of which very little is known, established by the Augustinian Friars in the Newport suburb. Thus there were five houses of friars in Lincoln in the thirteenth century, besides the monks and canons whom we have already described. No wonder the parish priests became alarmed. The friars were good preachers, especially the Dominicans. Their churches were large, and rich and poor were made welcome and invited to confess their sins and make their offerings. No wonder the parish priests called the friars "foxes" and their parishioners, who went to hear them, "geese."

THE HOSPITALS.
THE MALANDRY.

Besides the above religious houses there were numerous hospitals in Lincoln. Perhaps the most interesting was the hospital for lepers founded probably by Remigius in the eleventh century. This was an age of religious revival. New monasteries, cathedrals and churches were springing up. Pilgrims were travelling the roads from one monastery to another on their way to sacred shrines, and thought was being given to the sick and helpless. It was an age of striking contrasts. On the one hand were castles full of armed knights ready at any moment for war with one another and for the pillage of the poor, immensely rich monasteries and cathedrals, and arrogant Norman nobles ; and on the other, hospitals for the sick and helpless and for pilgrims on their pious journeys. Supporting it all were the villeins, tied to the soil, and unable to move from their place of birth because they belonged, like the cattle, to their lord's estate.

The age was cruel, and also kind. It was pious, and at the same time corrupt. This will be seen in the history of the Lepers' Hospital. If, as we are told, Remigius founded it before 1094, then it is probably the earliest in England. It was called the Hospital of the Holy Innocents, or more frequently " The Malandry," and stood just outside the ancient city walls, close to Little Bargate, on an oblong patch of ground known as the Malandry Closes, surrounded by the common land. The word Malandry comes from a French word meaning a 'house for the sick,' and it was set apart for the use of lepers, of whom there were many in the twelfth century. Leprosy existed in England in Saxon times. It may have been caused by the dirt, and salted meat, and badly made bread, and by the dirty habits of those days. By 1400 it was rare, but it lingered in Cornwall until the seventeenth century.

The Seal of the Malandry

The disease was regarded as a punishment for sin, and anyone suspected of suffering from it was brought before an inquest and carefully examined. If he was found to have contracted it, he was taken to the church by the priest and exhorted to bear his affliction in the true spirit of penitence. The priest then sprinkled him with holy water, clothed him in a black gown, and solemnly cut him off from the community of mankind, as though he were already dead. He was then led to his new abode, where he was solemnly forbidden to enter any church, mill, or bakehouse, to address strangers, to touch merchandise for sale, or wash in a running stream. He was given a rattle with which to warn passers-by of his approach, a shovelful of earth was thrown on his feet, and he was left to the care of his fellow sufferers.

Remigius is said to have given the hospital a revenue of 13 marks (£8 13s. 4d.) and Henry I endowed it for the maintenance of ten lepers of either sex, with a warden and two chaplains to say mass for the souls of the king and of his family, and a clerk to serve in the church of the hospital.

The gallows at Canwick formed one source of income for the Malandry. The law did not provide for the burial of criminals executed there, but the master of Maltby, a house belonging to the Hospitallers, as an act of charity, paid the leper house to bury them. The hospital even obtained one inmate from the gallows. About 1280, Mistress Margaret Everard of Burgh near Skegness, was hanged there for sheltering her son Richard, who was a thief. When she was believed to be dead, she was cut down and removed to the leper churchyard for burial, but she "was seen to draw a breath and revive." Her recovery was regarded as a miracle, and she was pardoned and allowed to live in the hospital.

When leprosy became uncommon people who were not suffering from any disease began to seek admission to the hospital, which provided safety and a living. In return for his patronage the king claimed the right to send to the hospital old servants or others whom he desired to reward at no cost to himself. In the reign of Henry VI it became necessary to make a rule that the hospital should not be burdened with more than three of the king's servants at a time. The master of the house sometimes accepted bribes from those who wished to enter the hospital. Simon de Barlings, who became the master in 1335, had nine brethren and sisters in the house, but only one was a leper and he paid Simon 100s. for his admission. The seven women in the house had also been admitted for payment. Time after time complaints were made that the lands and possessions of the hospital were wasted by the wardens, and repeatedly the king was obliged to settle disputes among the inmates. In 1284, the house was even placed under the custody of the sheriff for a time. Occasionally the bishops authorised collections in the churches for the hospital, but its finances were a constant source of trouble.   In 1327 the mayor was ordered to help to collect rents due to the Malandry.   In 1422 we hear that the books, goods and vestments of the hospital had been wasted by past wardens, and finally, in 1461, the Lincoln hospital was joined with the great leper house at Burton Lazars in Leicestershire.   The vicarage of St. Botolph's parish now stands on part of the site of the hospital.   The small triangular field fenced off from the South Common, and bounded on the north west by the railway line, was part of the Malandry Closes.

THE HOSPITAL OF THE HOLY SEPULCHRE.

The Hospital of the Holy Sepulchre was founded by Robert Bloet, second bishop of Lincoln (1094-1123).   It was intended for the sick, the poor, and orphan children.   When St. Catherine's Priory was founded by Bishop Chesney, the existing hospital was placed in the custody of the new priory, though the lay brethren continued to hold their own estates.   The main burden of supporting the inmates appears to have been met by sending out collectors to seek alms for the hospital.   Not infrequently unauthorised collectors caused trouble.   In 1309 the archdeacons of the diocese were warned against such rogues, and in 1329 the king ordered all sheriffs and bailiffs to arrest them. The hospital continued its work until the priory was closed.

St. Giles' Hospital.   Demolished in 1927

THE HOSPITAL OF ST. GILES.

The Hospital of St. Giles stood on the north side of Wragby Road, opposite Curle Avenue. It is first mentioned in 1280, but an unsupported tradition associates Remigius with its foundation. The vicars of the cathedral were closely connected with this hospital. They were required to keep chaplains there, and weak and infirm vicars were to be admitted to live there. In the fourteenth century the hospital endowments were increased by Gilbert d'Umfraville in order that aged cathedral servants might be admitted in preference to other applicants. Richard de Ravenser, Archdeacon of Lincoln, ordered that twelve such pensioners should be supported in the hospital and be given $\frac{1}{2}$d. daily for food, and four shillings yearly for clothes. This arrangement was confirmed by the dean and chapter in 1384. Several bequests to the hospital appear in local wills. The hospital did not cease to exist at the Reformation, but it became the custom to allow the bedesmen to live outside the hospital. In the middle of the nineteenth century five men were still receiving pensions. An image, believed to represent St. Giles, was found on the site of the hospital and is now preserved in the cathedral. The chief remaining fragments of the buildings were demolished in 1927.

Little is known of the other Lincoln hospitals. St. Bartholomew's is said to have been a refuge for converted Jews. After 1290 it would receive few inmates of this class and it is last mentioned in 1331.

St. Leonard's Hospital is said to have been

Statue in the Cathedral from the Hospital of St. Giles

founded as a leper hospital but probably received other sick persons. In 1300 and 1311 efforts were made by the bishop to assist its finances, but it appears to have been closed during the fourteenth century.

CHAPTER XIII.

DAYS OF DECLINE.

So far the story of Lincoln has been one of brilliant prosperity, gradually fading into a humdrum struggle and even into poverty, and as the city became poorer it also became smaller. The area remained the same of course, and the many large buildings and churches remained—but they were like a fine suit of clothes on an old shrunken man. The number of people had gone down from roughly 6,000 in the time of Domesday to less than 2,000 in the fifteenth century, and the busy life of the medieval city was at an end. It was so poor that again and again it had to beg for a reduction of its taxes—and sometimes they were remitted altogether. In 1441 Henry VI allowed the city to export to Calais 60 sacks of wool free of tax. Merchants and craftsmen deserted the town. In 1447 it was said scarcely 200 citizens dwelt there, and the king freed the city from the payment of tenths and fifteenths for 40 years. In 1463 Edward IV reduced the fee farm rent of the city from £180 to £80, and in 1466 the villages of Branston, Waddington, Brace-bridge and Canwick were annexed to the city, with the duty of contributing to the rates and taxes. We may be sure that all this help was not given to the city without good reason. Shortly after 1547, as we shall see, the number of parishes in the city was reduced to thirteen because so many had fallen into ruin and decay. The dead were buried in the churchyards of the ruined churches and marriages were solemnised at the deserted altars, but there was not money to maintain a priest, and parish life gradually ceased.

What can be the reason for this remarkable change ? Perhaps we should do better to ask just why Lincoln ever became prosperous at all. Possibly her early prosperity was built upon unstable foundations that would not stand the test of time.

One reason for Lincoln's importance was her military position, which commanded important routes. A strong garrison and castle would attract merchants and also would no doubt help to account for the favour which the king extended to Lincoln, and which played such an important part in the city's progress—but with the growth of settled national government this advantage would gradually disappear, and what the king had granted the king could take away. The change to more peaceful conditions made possible the growth of rivals such as Boston, which had the advantage of direct access to the open sea, and the king's favour ebbed and flowed, as always, in the wake of trade. With growing poverty it became more and more difficult to keep open the navigation of the Witham and the Fossdyke, and when this stopped the last advantage of Lincoln as a trading centre disappeared. Finally there came the great events in the last decade of the 15th century, which were to change not only the history of Lincoln, but the history of the world. In 1492 Columbus discovered America. In 1498 Vasco da Gama sailed round the Cape to India. What have these events to do with Lincoln? A great deal. Formerly Lincolnshire had been part of the great world. It had traded with every known region from the Baltic to the Mediterranean, and strangers from every country in Europe had sought its shores. But now the world was profoundly changed. The Mediterranean was no longer the centre, and as for the Baltic, it had become a back water. Not merely Lincoln, but Boston also was condemned to take a secondary place, while London and Bristol, Plymouth and Exeter, Southampton and Liverpool were to stride forward to the front in the struggle for oceanic trade. For three hundred years, from 1500 to 1800, the once brilliant city of Lincoln sinks into the position of a quiet market town whose torpor is only broken by the recurrent seasons of the year, by the bustle of markets and fairs, the assizes, the sessions, the petty excitements of corrupt elections, and the bickerings of rival religious bodies. But, as we shall see, there were still great events to come, and the conflicts that in the sixteenth and seventeenth centuries shook the nation were felt in Lincoln, too, and sometimes were fought out to the bitter end in its narrow streets and in the lanes and fields of the Lincolnshire countryside.

CHAPTER XIV.

THE PERIOD OF THE REFORMATION.

THE LINCOLNSHIRE REBELLION.

The accession of Henry VII in 1485 did nothing to cure Lincoln's troubles. On the contrary Henry himself seems to have regarded the city with something like disfavour, for it was not until 1498 that he confirmed its ancient privileges. We should remember the Earls of Lincoln had taken the part of the Yorkists in the Wars of the Roses, and though the town itself had shown no enthusiasm for either side, the mind of the new king was not inclined in its favour.

But an important event was impending which was to cause a great upheaval in the life of the city. In 1535 King Henry VIII dissolved the smaller monasteries—those with an income of less than £200 a year—and great dissatisfaction was felt in the country districts where the monks were, if not popular, at least less obnoxious than the new landlords who were buying up their land. About the same time the king's chancellor, Cromwell, had introduced compulsory registration of births and deaths, which aroused much suspicion in the minds of the people. But the gentry were even more dissatisfied than the common people, because they hated Cromwell and the new men who were coming in, frequently from London and other towns, to snap up the monastic lands.

They had been stirring up the commons for months, and so had the priests who were afraid that the protestant reformation which had started in Germany would sweep over England and carry them away. All kinds of rumours were circulated to enrage the common people, for without the strong arms of the commonalty neither priests nor gentry could do anything. Above all, the people were afraid their churches were going to be stripped by the king's commissioners, and when on October 2nd the proctor and registrar of the bishop of Lincoln arrived in Louth for the purpose of assessing the benefice with a view to levying further taxation, the people rose and imprisoned them. This was the signal for outbreaks in many parts of the county. Yorkshire was also rising and messages of encouragement were sent from the commoners of Beverley to the commoners of Lincolnshire. From Louth, Horncastle, and other Lincolnshire towns the rebels converged on Lincoln, 25,000 strong. They stopped at "Myle Cross, toward Netlame," probably at a point half way between Nettleham and Lincoln, and discussed their grievances afresh and drew up a revised list of articles, which was copied out by Sir Edward Maddison and sent to the king. They demanded, among other things, that the king should change his advisers. A week later the king's reply was received. The leaders of the rebels, Sir Robert Tyrwhit, Sir William Skipworth, Sir William Ascough, Sir Edward Maddison and other gentlemen, were assembled in the chapter house to hear it, but three hundred of the commons forced their way into the cathedral and insisted on joining them. The commons suspected that the gentlemen might wish to play them false. Nerves were strained and tempers were rising. Thomas Moigne, the recorder of the city, began to read the letter, and he soon came to the passage in which the king said, " I have never read, heard, nor known that Prince's Counsellors and Prelates should be appoynted by rude and ignorant people ; nor that they were persons mete or of ability, to discern and choose mete and sufficient counsellors for a Prince. How presumptious then are ye, the rude commons of one shire and that one of the most brute and beastly of the whole realm and of least experience, to find fault with your Prince for the electing of his Counsellors and Prelates." Thomas Moigne tactfully omitted part of this royal outburst. As he explained afterwards "there was a lyttel clause therein that we feared wolde styr the commons. I did leav that clause unredd." Unfortunately the omission was perceived by the parson of Snelland who said openly that the letter was falsely read. The suspicious commons were roused. They thought the gentry were plotting to deceive them and withdrew to the cloister to decide what to do. Should they kill the gentry there and then in the chapter house, from which there was no escape, or give them another chance on the morrow to go forward with the commons? They decided to leave them alone for the night, but at the west door of the cathedral they changed their minds and were for going back to kill them as they came out. But the gentlemen had called their servants about them, and with their help they escaped through the south door into the chancellor's house ; but the commons promised to have their lives next day.

The rising was now doomed. The gentlemen—who were afterwards described to Cromwell as "a sight of asses . . . void of good fashion, and, in truth of wit"—deserted the commons, and waited in the Close to be rescued by the king's troops. The commons were downhearted, and when Thomas Myller, Lancaster Herald of Arms, who had been sent by the king with a proclamation to Lincoln, called a meeting—possibly at the castle gate—and made them a persuasive speech, most of them agreed to go home and leave the gentlemen to sue for their pardon. The king sent a further proclamation to the rebels offering to pardon all who "will in peaceable sort leave all your harness and all your other weapons in the market place of that our city of Lincoln," and go home ; and threatening to "execute all extremity against you, your wives and children without mercy" if they continued one whole day longer in rebellion. By Friday night (October 14th) the city was quiet and the rising was over. But the rebels at Beverley were still in arms. When a messenger brought the news that the Lincolnshire men had gone home, the commons cried that the letter was a forgery and the man a liar. What might not have happened if Lincolnshire had stood by the men of the north ?

The unfortunate Thomas Moigne, who had read the letter in the chapter house, Lord Hussey and other leaders, were tried the next year and "hanged, headed, drawn, and quartered." Fifteen persons were handed over at Louth to the Earl of Shrewsbury, and the king sent orders that, in case of any renewed attempt by the commons, the Earl's forces "shall run before them with all extremity and burn and kill man, woman, and child, to the terrible example of all others, especially the town of Louth because the rebellion took a beginning with same."

So ended the Lincolnshire rising, and with it the last opportunity to check the progress of the religious revolution and restrain the terrible will of Henry VIII.

RELIGIOUS PERSECUTION.

But the suppression of the rebellion does not mark the end of religious conflict. Beneath the peaceful surface which Henry had imposed by force and terror, there was a deep conflict of opinion that could not be hidden. Henry had broken with the pope, dissolved the monasteries, and even despoiled the churches, but he was not a protestant. There were many who wished to go further and change the doctrine as well as the government of the church. One of the most interesting of the local advocates of reform was Anne Askew, the " Fair Gospeller," a native of Stallingborough, who came to Lincoln to challenge the clergy themselves. Every day for a week she stood by the lectern, and read from the Bible that was chained there in accordance with the order of Henry VIII, and tried to draw her audiences, clergy and laymen alike, into discussion. " I went thydre in dede," she said in her confession later, "not beying afrayed because I knew my matter to be good." She was advocating an extreme form of Protestantism—Presbyterianism—according to which the bishops were unnecessary, and the people of Lincoln had no desire to be associated with such dangerous doctrines, and refused to be drawn into controversy with her. She went to London, was arrested, released and arrested again. She had sought and found martyrdom, but though she was tortured on the rack and finally burnt, her courage never faltered.

There was equal courage on the opposite side. All through the reigns of Henry VIII, Edward VI, and Mary, the religious conflicts had burned more and more fiercely ; but the majority of the people were still Catholic at the accession of Elizabeth in 1558. She decided as far as possible, to take a middle course, and in so doing saved the country from the disaster of civil war. But neither side was content. The Catholics plotted in support of Mary Queen of Scots. The Protestants wished to go further in the direction of Presbyterianism, and it was realised by all that the life of Queen Elizabeth alone stood between the country and civil war. When Philip of Spain took up the quarrel after Mary's execution in 1587 many Catholics came over to Elizabeth's side because they feared foreign conquest even more than the triumph of the Protestant faith ; but some Catholics put their faith before their patriotism and took the side of Spain. The result was that Catholics—especially Catholic priests—were regarded as traitors and fierce acts were passed against them. Catholic priests were forbidden to live in England at all. If they were found they were liable to be treated as traitors and executed. A Lincoln priest, Roger Dickenson, was executed at Winchester under the act in 1591. Two priests who were found in the Saracen's

Photograph by)   (Lincolnshire Echo

THE CATHEDRAL CHAPTER HOUSE

Head at Lincoln were arrested in 1600. They had committed no offence except belonging to a proscribed faith ; but the law had to run its course. The jury, before whom they were tried, reluctantly brought in a verdict of guilty, and the two unfortunate men were hanged, drawn and quartered on Canwick Hill.

In spite of this terrible example, Catholics continued to practise their religion in secret. All through the period of the Reformation and the persecution of Elizabeth, the Catholic community continued to exist.

CHAPTER XV.

THE REFORMATION AND THE CHURCHES.

We must now notice some further examples of the effects of the Reformation in Lincoln.

As we have seen the monasteries and friaries had been closed, first St. Catherine's in 1538, then the friaries in 1539, and finally the cell now known as Monks' Abbey.

No doubt these events caused much excitement and discussion in the city, but in 1540 the treasures of the cathedral itself were seized by the king. Although the age of pilgrimages had passed and the city no longer made great profits from the hundreds of pilgrims who had formerly visited the shrines of saints in the cathedral, the citizens would still be proud of the magnificence and beauty of such shrines as those of St. Hugh, Little St. Hugh, and Bishop Dalderby.

No doubt there would be many heavy hearts in the city when it became certain that what the men of Louth had feared would happen to their church in 1536, was about to happen to Lincoln Cathedral.

A letter was received from Henry VIII, saying that he had heard of the existence at Lincoln of the shrines and pretended relics whereby "all the people be much deceived and brought into great superstition and idolatry." He then declared that he had determined to bring his "loving subjects to the right knowledge of the truth by taking away all occasions of idolatry and superstition" and ordered that the shrines, "superstitious relics, superfluous jewels, plate, copes and other such like" should immediately be "safely and surely conveyed to our Tower of London into our Jewel House."

His orders were obeyed. Over 4,000 ozs. of silver and 2,631 ozs. of gold, besides a great number of pearls, diamonds, rubies and other precious stones went into the king's treasury. When Harry Lytherland, the last treasurer of the cathedral, saw them carried out, he flung down his keys on the pavement of the choir and cried, " Ceasing the Treasure, so ceaseth the office of Treasurer."

A great image of the Virgin and many "superstitious relics" were removed. The relics included a finger of St. Catherine, a tooth of St. Paul, and a bone of St. Stephen.

A few articles of value were left, but shortly after Henry VIII died, Henry Holbeach became Bishop of Lincoln. He was a keen reformer and willing to please the king, to whom he surrendered many rich manors belonging to the see of Lincoln. This impoverished the bishop's successors so much that they ceased to maintain their palace at Lincoln and made their home at Nettleham, and later at Buckden. In Edward VI's reign (1548) Bishop Holbeach and Dean Heneage caused many of the carved tombs in the cathedral to be destroyed, and pulled down the figures of the saints.

Five years earlier in 1543, Dean Heneage had not been such an ardent reformer. He had then been engaged in making arrangements for founding a new chantry in the chapel on the High Bridge. This chapel had been built in the thirteenth century and was dedicated to St. Thomas the Martyr, *i.e.*, Thomas Becket. The mayor and council appointed the priest and were responsible for the chapel's maintenance. Dean Heneage gave the city £100 on the understanding that the city should found a chantry for him in the chapel at

High Bridge Chapel

the end of seven years. The priest was to have a yearly salary of £5. Before the seven years were over the Reformation had swept away chantries and the chapel had ceased to be used for religious purposes. A sum of £40 was returned to the dean.

In 1549 the bells of the chapel were removed and sold, and the building was converted into a dwellinghouse. Twenty years later it became the hall of the Company of Tanners and Butchers. It was pulled down shortly before 1763 and an obelisk was erected in its place, which in its turn was removed in 1939.

There had been more than 20 chantries in the cathedral, some served by a single priest, others such as the Burghersh, Cantilupe, and Works chantries, by a group of priests having their own house near the cathedral. These priests celebrated masses and offered prayers for the souls of the founders of their chantries and others.

The Burghersh chantry was founded by Bartholomew Burghersh, at the altar of St. Catherine near the north east corner of the Angel Choir, where we can still see his tomb, and those of his father, Robert, and his brother, Henry. Bartholomew was present at the battle of Crecy. Henry was Bishop of Lincoln, and Treasurer and Chancellor of England. He has been described as "eminent only for disloyalty to his prince, and oppressing the poor," though he gained some fame as a statesman and is described by another writer as "greatly renowned . . . both in wisdom and prowess." He baptised the Black Prince. The house in James Street where the priests of the chantry lived is still known as the Burghersh Chantry.

At the eastern end of the south aisle of the Angel Choir is the Cantilupe chantry chapel. This chantry was founded by Joan, the widow of Nicholas de Cantilupe, to be served by a warden and seven chaplains. Their house still stands near the entrance to Vicars' Court.

The chantry in the High Bridge chapel, the chantries in the cathedral, and many in the parish churches, were closed early in the reign of Edward VI. After a short delay many of the priests who had served the chantries were granted pensions. In 1555, Robert Bowker, formerly a priest of the Hugh Welles chantry in the cathedral, was receiving £6 6s. 6d. a year. Four of the Burghersh chantry priests, two formerly serving the Cantilupe chantry, and two of the Works chantry priests, were each receiving £6. This amount was little less than was considered sufficient at that time for the needs of a clergyman with full parish duties.

Other priests were not so fortunate. Thomas Goodnappe the priest of the Gild of St. Anne received £4, and William Smith, who had served the Tattershall chantry in St. Benedict's church received £3 17s. 2d.

The chantry priests were by no means the only clergy who were deprived of their offices in these troubled times. Even bishops were far from secure if they ventured to express opinions which

offended the sovereign for the time being. John Taylor who
succeeded Henry Holbeach as bishop, was a firm protestant and
was removed from his office by Queen Mary, whilst John Watson
who was made bishop by Mary was removed by Queen Elizabeth
and imprisoned for many years.

The parish churches, of course, were greatly affected by the
changes in religion. Not only were their ornaments removed, and
the chantries in them closed, but the incomes of the parish priests
were much reduced. At one time Lincoln had been served by about
fifty churches. The removal of the staple to Boston and the depression in trade caused by great pestilence had caused many
parishes to be almost deserted. As far back as 1263 it was evident
that Lincoln had more parish churches than it needed, and the
parishes of St. Faith and St. Mary le Wigford had been united.
Other unions of parishes took place at intervals, and when the
monasteries and friaries were dissolved some of their inhabitants
appear to have supplemented their pensions by acting as priests in
impoverished parishes. In 1549 an act for enabling the mayor and
bishop to unite parishes in Lincoln was passed. It tells us that the
income of some of the city clergy was "not above the clear yearly
value of 30s.," and that "of poverty and necessity there are divers
late religious persons . . . appointed to serve the benefices, which
for the most part are unlearned and very ignorant persons, not able
to do any part of their duties." The parishes were united so that
the incomes of the newly formed parishes were about £7 10s. a year.
The city authorities were given power to pull down unwanted
churches and sell the building material or use it for the repair of
other churches or of bridges within the city. The money obtained
from the sale of material might be used for the relief of the poor.
The number of parishes was reduced to thirteen, and all the re-
arrangement was completed by 1553.

During the Civil Wars the churches suffered very severely, and at the Restoration only three remained fit for public worship. These were St. Mary le Wigford, St. Peter at Arches, and St. Peter-at-Gowts, and of these St. Peter at Arches was rebuilt in the eighteenth century, only to be demolished in 1933. After the Restoration the church of St. Benedict was made serviceable again by pulling down the nave and rebuilding the tower close to the chancel. Bracebridge has now been brought within the city boundary, and possesses an ancient church. If we wish to study examples of medieval architecture in the parish churches of Lincoln it is to these churches that we must go. We shall find towers of a late Saxon type at each of the four surviving churches, and Saxon "long and short" work at the corners of the nave of Bracebridge church and at the original western corners of the nave in the church of St. Peter-at-

ORDINARY
COIGNING.

SAXON · LONG-AND-
SHORT WORK·

Gowts. Perhaps the most interesting church in the city is that of St. Benedict which contains some good fourteenth and fifteenth century work, including a fine east window.

But we must return to our story of the Reformation period in Lincoln. The union of the parishes had been completed in the reign of Mary, and under her the old services were restored and many of the former ornaments of the churches were replaced. Her reign, however, was short and under Elizabeth the churches were again stripped of images and "popish implements." A list of such articles removed from St. Paul's church has been preserved. It was

St. Benedict church is now the headquarters of the Mothers' Union.

drawn up in 1566 and tells us that the images had been burnt ; the mass book removed by "our parson" ; the rood loft, candlesticks, bells, and pix broken up and sold ; banner cloths, vestments, "and all such linen trumpery" cut in pieces and sold ; the altar stones used for paving the church ; and other articles "gone we know not how or when." The churches must have looked very bare to the people who had been accustomed to the rich colouring and ornaments of earlier days. The Elizabethan settlement brought an end to the violent changes of the Reformation period but it did not bring religious agreement.

CHAPTER XVI.

THE CIVIL WARS.

The religious difficulties which we have seen in Elizabeth's reign became more serious, and the split between the Anglicans and those who wanted greater simplicity became deeper. The spirit of puritanism was especially strong in the towns, and Boston, Grimsby and Stamford all sent reformers to the parliament of 1640—the famous Long Parliament that rebelled against Charles I and eventually executed him. The country districts, too, were affected, and it is estimated that at least half the nobility, and probably more than half the farmers, favoured a reform of the church. Lincoln itself was divided. A few still clung to the Catholic faith. Even through the severe persecutions of Elizabeth and James they met in secret to worship in their own way, and with the coming of Charles and his Catholic wife, Henrietta Maria, they became bolder. The corporation, however, was distinctly puritan, and as early as 1583 they appointed a city preacher, or a lecturer as he was sometimes called, at a salary of £20 a year, to hold services of a puritanical kind. It is possible that even the cathedral, too, was affected by this powerful movement towards greater simplicity in church service. At any rate, soon after Charles I came to the throne, Bishop John Williams quarrelled with Archbishop Laud, who was trying to compel the clergy to introduce more elaborate ritual and to suppress the Puritans, and when he refused to pay a heavy and unjust tax which Charles' government imposed upon him, he was imprisoned.

We can imagine the feeling aroused in Lincoln when a bishop opposed the king's religious policy, and was imprisoned for refusing

to pay the king's illegal taxes. Men took their religion with a
seriousness we can hardly understand today, and they were furious
when not only their consciences but their pockets were attacked.
The king was making enemies for himself on all sides. He was
imposing heavy and unjust taxes on the rich. He punished landlords with heavy fines for enclosing the common and for putting
down arable to pasture (though he encouraged enclosure when it
suited him). He supported Archbishop Laud in his High Church
policy, and when Parliament protested he dismissed it, and ruled
alone for eleven years—the "eleven years tyranny" as it is sometimes
called. The only people who seemed pleased with him were the
Catholics. They were winning great victories abroad in the Thirty
Years' War, and Protestants in England became more and more
alarmed. Did Charles intend to restore Catholicism? He had a
Catholic wife, and priests were appearing again openly in the streets
of London. No doubt they flitted nervously about Lincoln, too.

But in favour of Charles I we should remember that though he
made enemies among the rich whom he taxed illegally and punished
heavily, he was a friend of the poor. Above all he tried to enforce
the Poor Law regulations of Elizabeth, and so provide relief for the
old and sick, and employment for the able bodied poor. He made
many mistakes. He broke his pledged word. He inflicted heavy
punishments on his opponents and he was an enemy of freedom,
but the burdens he imposed upon his people fell mainly on those
who could bear them best, the landowners and merchants. Can we
wonder that they clamoured for the calling of Parliament? Only if
Parliament met would they be able to keep a check on the king.

At last it met, in 1640, and all the representatives from Lincolnshire were in favour of reform. They were followers of Pym and
Cromwell, and were anxious to reform the church as well as to
control the king. Many laws were passed limiting the king's power,

but when the question of the church arose there was a split, but not among the Lincolnshire members. They were unanimously with the Puritans against the king and church, but in Lincoln itself there was a great debate and deep division. Even families were divided against themselves, brother against brother, and father against son. There were advantages as well as disadvantages in this, however, as we see in the case of the family of Becke. Robert Becke, woollen draper, was mayor in 1640, and a Royalist; but his son, John, who was also his partner in business was a supporter of Parliament. Out of an aldermanic bench of thirteen the Parliamentarians had seven, and they expelled the father for being a Royalist and fined him £60, but the son continued to sit until the Restoration, when he, in his turn, was expelled for being a Parliamentarian. But the family had been represented on the Council for twenty troubled years. Many of the gentry had houses in Lincoln—Monson, Heneage, Meres, Dallison, Neal, Whichcote, Lister, Willoughby, Tyrwhit, Lake, Grantham, Hatcher, and Disney, and they, like the Council, were almost equally divided.

The great question of this time was the control of the militia, or trained bands. If the king secured control, he might be able to drive out Parliament and rule by force. In order to avoid this the Lords Lieutenants, who were in command of the militia, were instructed to look for orders to Parliament alone, and not to the king. Lord Willoughby of Parham was Lord Lieutenant of Lindsey, and later of the whole county of Lincoln. He was a reformer in religion and a strong supporter of Parliament, and he took prompt measures to muster the trained bands and secure their support. It was not long before he received a letter from the king ordering him to cease these activities on pain of being brought strictly to account for his disobedience. To this he replied that he held his authority from Parliament, which was considered by most learned lawyers to be the supreme authority. If he was mistaken in this, he begged that his want of years—he was thirty—would excuse his conduct. Nothing he had done had any other end than to promote the honour and safety of his Majesty's Person, and the preservation of the peace of the kingdom. Lord Willoughby was a reluctant traitor. He honoured the king while defying his authority. It is sad to think that they could not settle their quarrels, so unwillingly entered into, and so courteously conducted, without war. How different are these deep but courtly differences from the furious enmities of today !

The Outer Exchequer Gate, known as " The Magazine House"
Demolished in 1796.

Lord Willoughby did not waver in his support of Parliament. He ordered the mayor to give up the keys of the Magazine of Arms in the Outer Exchequer Gate. The mayor gave up the keys, but, frightened at what he had done, fled to York and made his peace with the king. Parliament's supporters drew up a Declaration in which they declared themselves ready to spend their lives and estates in defence of his Majesty's person, the Protestant religion, the Rights and Privileges of Parliament and the peace of the realm. It was sent through Lord Willoughby to Parliament in the name of the Knights, Gentry and Freeholders of Lincolnshire, and attested by "many thousands" both great and small. Lord Willoughby was busy enrolling volunteers and training them on the fields round the town. He was also making preparations to receive troops of horse from the south. The war clouds were rolling round Lincoln, and the Royalists begged the king to visit the city in the hope that his presence might dispel them. On 13th July, 1642, he came, and if a Royalist tract printed at the time is to be believed, he was received with enthusiasm. For four miles, it was said there was a throng of people who received the king with shouts of joy. The gentry drew their swords to show they were willing, if necessary, to use them on his enemies, and the clergy, estimated at between two and three hundred, redoubled the shouts of welcome. Among those who waited on Charles, there was not one Papist of any note, but it was also pointed out that not one in twenty of the crowd had so much as a sword about them. They had come to stare ; they were willing to shout ; but they showed no inclination to fight. The town of Hull had openly defied the king, and Lincoln was fearful that it might be asked to battle against a neighbour who was also a good customer. Although the Catholics of Lincolnshire were not prominent in his support at this time, the king was accepting money from Catholics to prepare for war, and within a month of his visit

to Lincoln he invited their armed assistance as well.   This does not,
of course, mean that he intended to betray the Protestant faith, but
we cannot be surprised that many earnest Puritans were deeply
suspicious and alarmed.

One result of the king's visit was that a loyal regiment was
raised in Lincolnshire to be kept within the county for three months.
Apparently the king's supporters did not anticipate a long struggle,
but after his departure enthusiasm for his cause waned.   William
Marshall, a strong Parliamentarian, was elected mayor and the city
passed into the hands of the king's opponents.

By this time the war had definitely begun.   The battle of
Edgehill had been fought, and it was only a matter of time before
the tide of war would roll over Lincoln.   The city lay near the
boundary of the districts occupied by the rival parties.   More
important still, Lincoln stood between the king's armies in the
north and the south, and was in a position to threaten any large
movement on London with attack in the rear.   Lincolnshire must
be won if the king was to regain the south.   From the summer of
1643 to the summer of 1644 the struggle went on, and for many
anxious months the issue lay in the balance.   Lincoln itself changed
hands more than once.   In July 1643 the Cavaliers, by means of a
clever ruse, succeeded in gaining an entrance.   Sixty of their supporters came disguised as country folk and were admitted to the city and
hidden in the Dean's house by Sergeant Major Purefoy, who was in
the plot.   At the same time, two thousand Royalists were sent
from Newark to lie in wait near the city until, by a pre-arranged
signal, they should be admitted.   But the plot miscarried.   Sergeant
Major Purefoy and his brother were arrested.   The Cavaliers in the
Dean's house sallied out and tried to seize the magazine in the
Outer Exchequer Gate, but a cannon was fired at them by a country-
man who had never fired a piece of artillery before, and they were

scattered. But the city's defences were too weak to withstand a serious attack, and Lord Willoughby withdrew his forces to Boston and allowed the Royalists to enter the city. They did not hold it long, for in October 1643 the battle of Winceby saved Lincolnshire for Parliament, and the Royalists surrendered the city without a blow. In March 1644 Prince Rupert won a victory at Newark and the Parliamentarians were seized with panic. They again left the city defenceless ; but on Friday the third of May the Earl of Manchester approached the city from Canwick, and entered it through Little Bargate. He seized the lower town and on the following Monday proceeded to storm the upper town and castle, to which the Royalists had fled. So serious was the onslaught that the defenders fled in terror, and some of them hid in the cathedral. The castle walls were scaled in the face of a hail of stones from the walls, but when the defenders saw how resolutely the attackers came on, they fled in panic, and not knowing where to run, cried out for quarter, saying that they were poor men who had been forced to fight.

After the victory the Roundheads were allowed to pillage the houses in the Close and upper town, and also the cathedral, but they spared the Bishop's Palace. They tore off the brasses on the tombstones, removed altar ornaments and pictures, and damaged the windows and even the sculptures, but the story that they stabled their horses in the cathedral rests on very insecure foundation. Lead was taken from the roofs of churches for bullets, and many houses were stripped of their water pipes.

From now until the second Civil War in 1648, Lincoln enjoyed a period of peace. In that year the Scots invaded England on behalf of Charles, and the Cavaliers seized Pontefract Castle, from which they made raids in all directions. Lincoln was defended by only 100 men, since all the rest had been sent to ward off a threatened attack upon the more important town of Newark. On June 30th news was brought that a body of four hundred horse and two hundred musketeers had crossed the Trent at Gainsborough and were marching on Lincoln. What could a hundred do against six hundred ? The only place capable of defence was the Bishop's Palace, which had walls sixteen feet high, and was strong enough, it was hoped, to stand a siege until help should come from Newark. The raiders made their headquarters in the cathedral, and after a three hours' siege, in which they set the palace on fire, the defenders surrendered. The blazing palace was then looted and left a smouldering ruin.

At this time, of course, the cathedral was no longer under the bishop's control. In 1643 the office of bishop had been abolished and the chapter dissolved. Their place was taken by preachers appointed by Parliament, and the use of the Prayer Book had been prohibited. A Presbyterian form of church service was used, and much stress laid on long prayers and still longer sermons, with little music and no ornamental aids to religious worship, such as robes, vestments, lighted candles and processions. A gloomy puritanism was thrust upon the people, even more forcibly than Charles had tried to turn all Englishmen into High Anglicans.

When the Royalists had sacked the Bishop's Palace, they soon had to retreat before superior forces under Colonel Rossiter. Peace returned at last and Lincoln had leisure to count her losses. The most serious was the damage done to the cathedral. The soldiers had knocked off the brass inscriptions from the gravestones, and broken the windows. It was even suggested that the cathedral should be pulled down so that several smaller "houses of God" could be built of the material, but the proposal was turned down

ST. PETER-AT-ARCHES CHURCH

(Demolished 1933)

by Cromwell after energetic protests by the mayor. Several parish churches, the castle, and many houses were also in ruins, especially the homes of leading supporters of either side, and it was only with the growth of trade and population in the eighteenth century that the scars of war were gradually removed.

But more important than damage to property was the bitterness that divided the opposing sections of the community, and the tendency to settle disputes by force rather than by the ordinary course of law. There is especially the case of the two Cromwellian soldiers who planned the murder of a fellow townsman of the opposite party for using a sporting gun against the Protector's orders, and the attempt of Major General Whalley to bully the judges into letting off the one found guilty of murder. But the judges passed sentence and hanged the murderer immediately to prevent any further interference with the course of the law. The Major General also interfered in local elections. He insisted that the Town Clerk's office should be given to his own nominee in order to enable the Cromwellians to obtain a majority on the council.

After the Restoration these decisions were reversed and the Royalists obtained a majority. The dean and chapter were restored to their offices, and also to their ruined houses in the Close ; a search was made for the missing books from the cathedral library ; their houses were repaired and they took their accustomed place in the life of the city. Their sufferings had not been severe. They had been provided for during the Civil Wars and Commonwealth, either by pensions or by receiving livings in other parts of the country. Their chief difficulty was found in obtaining the restoration of property belonging to the chapter which had been bought by private individuals, but the question was soon settled by the ordinary process of law. In twenty years the wheel had gone full circle. A revolution had taken place, the first of the great revolutions of modern history—but how mild and humane in comparison with the horrors we read about today. Can we be sure that men have progressed in the last three hundred years ?

CHAPTER XVII.

THE RISE OF NONCONFORMITY.

There was one change made in the life of Lincoln during the period of the Civil Wars and the Commonwealth which has lasted to our own day. That was the rise of nonconformist bodies, especially the Quakers, Baptists and Congregationalists, separate from the Anglican Church, with their own organisations and meeting places. The split had begun, as we have seen, in Elizabeth's reign when special preachers were appointed by the corporation, additional to those of the cathedral and the parish churches, to instruct the people in their duties to God and the Queen. They preached on Wednesday as well as Sunday and the people had to go to listen to them whether they liked it or not. Every household had to be represented at the Sunday sermon and the weekday sermon on the pain of 20d. for absence on Sunday and 12d. on the week day. The fines grew heavier as time went on, which suggests that regular attendance was unpopular. The preachers became more definitely Puritan in their views, and one of them, Mr. John Smith, left the city in 1602, and in 1606 we find him at the head of a Baptist congregation in Gainsborough. No doubt he had left many sympathisers behind him in Lincoln, for a Baptist church certainly existed in 1626. It was led by lay preachers who were hated both by Anglicans and Puritans. "They have bold foreheads, strong lungs and talk loud," said Bishop Williams. "An empty cask will make a great sound if you knock upon it, yet a world of unstable people flock after these coachmen-preachers, watchmaking-preachers, barber-preachers and such addle-headed companions." Religious democracy was evidently very distasteful to the bishop.

He does not seem to have objected to Puritan clergymen, however. In 1626 Edward Reyner was appointed as lecturer at St. Benedict's Church, and the next year as Rector of St. Peter at Arches, and although he was opposed to the ceremonies of the Anglican Church, he was allowed to preach for many years, and take a leading part in the religious life of the city. When the Royalists entered the city he fled for his life, but in 1645 he was persuaded, very reluctantly, to come back and continue his work. Among his opponents was a new sect, the Quakers, who abused Reyner for receiving payment for his ministrations.

The growth of the Quakers dates from the visit of George Fox in 1654. He made many converts, including one of the sheriffs of the city. The members of the sect were usually found among the smaller tradesmen, artisans and farmers. They were intensely unpopular and one of their number would have been murdered by the mob but for the interference of the Cromwellian soldiers who were in the town.

After the Restoration, all nonconformist sects were severely persecuted. In 1662 the Act of Uniformity was passed, and many ministers either left their livings or were turned out. The Conventicle Act prevented them from meeting in private houses, and the Five Mile Act prohibited preachers from coming within five miles of a corporate town where they had formerly preached. But the Quakers continued to meet openly regardless of consequences. They were imprisoned in Lincoln Castle gaol and there were so many of them that they were allowed a separate room, and a loom on which they might work and earn money for their necessities. Prisoners in those days, we should remember, had to pay their board ! The other nonconformist bodies obtained licences to open their meeting houses, but this the Quakers refused to do.

The nonconformists were greatly encouraged when the king, in order to give freedom to the Roman Catholics, issued his Declaration of Indulgence and suspended the laws against them. Numerous conventicles, or chapels, as we should say, at once sprang into existence, and though the king later tried to undo the work he had done, the nonconformist movement was now established. In 1689, a year after the Revolution which drove away the Catholic James and established William of Orange on the throne, the Toleration Act was passed. From this time nonconformists could meet freely if they obtained a certificate from the bishop of the diocese,

Interior of the Old Meeting House of the Lincoln Society of Friends

and in this year the Quakers built the meeting house in Park Street, which is now the oldest nonconformist building in Lincoln.

Although the nonconformists were free to worship, they were rigidly excluded from political power. The council was in the hands of Tories, Anglicans to a man, who took good care not to allow a nonconformist among them. Quakers were prevented from becoming freemen because they would not take the necessary oath, as the case of Abraham Morrice shows. He had served seven years as apprentice to a mercer, and was qualified to become a freeman. James II claimed the right to excuse his subjects from taking an oath, and decided to use his "dispensing power" in favour of Morrice. The mayor and council were obliged to admit him as a freeman, but when William III became king, Morrice was expelled from the freedom.

A remarkable change now came over the nonconformist movement, and indeed over religious life in general. Having obtained the right to worship as they pleased, many nonconformists lost their desire to worship at all. A strange torpor fell upon church and chapel alike, and it was not until John Wesley established the Methodist movement that they were restored to new life.

The Methodist movement had made great progress throughout the country before it penetrated Lincoln. Even in the villages around the city there were active groups at work, but none inside. At last the city fell to the attack of two women, Sarah Parrot of Bracebridge and Mrs. Fisher of Gonerby. From her Methodist class at Sturton, which was nine miles away, Sarah Parrot walked to Gonerby, twenty-seven miles away, in order to persuade Mrs. Fisher, a devout Methodist, to take a house in Lincoln and to form a Methodist Society. Not even Lincoln could withstand such zeal. The Society, consisting of four women, met in a lumber room near Gowt's Bridge, and two years later the first Wesleyan Meeting House was built in the yard of Mrs. Fisher's house, in Meanwell Court, which stood on Waterside South to the north of the Central Market. On July 1st, 1790, shortly after the Meeting House had been opened, it received a visit from the great evangelist himself, John Wesley, now in his 90th year. He had toured England again and again in his marvellous career, and had preached in Lincoln twice before, but he had always found it "a soil unfruitful to the tiller's toil." It now began to bear fruit. In 1815 a new chapel was built in Bank Street where the Lincoln Savings Bank now stands. This was followed in 1836 by the present Methodist Chapel in Clasketgate, still the biggest centre of nonconformity in the city.

The Thomas Cooper Memorial Chapel was built on the site of an earlier Baptist Church and named after a famous poet, teacher, preacher, journalist, and politician. He came to Lincoln in 1834. He was the first teacher of languages at the Mechanics' Institute, and a keen fighter for the poor and oppressed. He became a leader of the Chartists, and was imprisoned for his speeches at Hanley in support of their movement. In 1849 he edited " Plain Speaking," one of the earliest newspapers to be devoted to the cause of the working classes. He returned to Lincoln about the year 1872, and died here in 1892.

It is difficult for us now to realise the part played by the non-conformist chapel in the lives of our grandfathers and great-grand-fathers. The chapel was the centre not only of religious life, but of social life and culture for the ordinary man. There were few schools. There were no sports clubs. Many modern amusements were not dreamed of. Above all, the chapels helped to educate their members by forming Sunday Schools. In 1809 the first Sunday School was opened in Lincoln, not by some leading preacher,

Methodist Chapel in Clasketgate was demolished in 1963.

Thomas Cooper Memorial Chapel will shortly be demolished and a new Chapel built on a site in High Street formerly occupied by Hannah Memorial Methodist Chapel which was demolished in 1965.

but by John Hannah, a boy of seventeen, the son of a Methodist merchant. It is possible there may have been a Sunday School as early as 1802, but the credit for starting the movement in Lincoln is generally given to John Hannah, in whose honour the chapel in High Street is named.

CHAPTER XVIII.

EDUCATION IN LINCOLN.

It is an astonishing thing that just over a century ago the poorer children of Lincoln were so utterly ignorant and neglected that a boy of seventeen took pity on them and hired a room at his own expense, in which he might teach them their letters. There were, of course, expensive "academies" for those who could pay, and a Grammar School for those who wished to learn Latin, but for the poor who wished to learn to read and write, there was nothing. This had not always been so. In the middle ages there was probably a certain amount—perhaps a good deal—of free education both elementary and secondary. For instance there were chantries in Lincoln founded by pious benefactors who had left land for their upkeep, and some at least of the chantry priests would teach the children of the men of the gild to which they were attached, and a great many children would learn to read and sing music in the choirs connected with the cathedral, and the numerous parish churches. There must have been several song schools in medieval Lincoln, and musical training in those days was very thorough. It meant an ability to take your part along with others in difficult part singing without accompaniment. How many of us could do that today? The people of the middle ages were ignorant of many things which the modern schoolboy knows, but they had a taste for art, architecture, music, beautiful writing and craftsmanship, as we can see for ourselves by their work in any of the older parts of Lincoln.

But a great blow was struck at popular education by the Reformation. Henry VIII dissolved the chantries and religious gilds and confiscated their property, and with the chantries went the schools and schoolmasters of the poor. That is one reason why John Hannah had to start a Sunday School.

If Henry VIII had used the money to set up elementary schools, as was done, for instance, in Scotland and in some parts of the continent, we should have had an educated people, and perhaps a singing people, today. We are getting them, now, in our schools, but the dreadful ignorance, almost barbarism, of the common people in the time of Wesley and John Hannah, and during a large part of the nineteenth century, might never have existed. The need for new schools was felt very urgently at this time, and many people tried to start little schools of their own—Dame schools in which the "Dames" often knew little more than the children they taught— Ragged schools, run by shoemakers, for instance, in their workshops. Gradually the movement for popular education became organised by two powerful societies, and they began to establish schools for the upper working class in Lincoln. A " National " School was established in 1813 in Silver Street. It was evidently a great success, for in 1833 it had 500 boys and girls in attendance. But the building left much to be desired. In 1881 one part of the building was described as "a mere dirty shed, a disgrace to the city, badly lighted, ill conceived, ill ventilated."

How could 400 to 500 children " eager and enthusiastic students "—for they *paid* to come—be taught in a school of this type ? The answer is, by means of the monitorial system, by which the scholars were divided into groups of ten or twenty and over each group a "monitor"—a child who was slightly more advanced than the children in the group—was placed, with the duty of hearing the children of the group repeat their lesson until they had got it by heart. We can imagine what kind of a noise would be coming from the school if we could have stood and listened to the twenty classes under their twenty monitors learning their tables, their spelling, their history dates, and the capes and bays of England by rote a century ago.

In 1833 the Government made its first grant to elementary education—a tardy return of the endowment which had been taken away from it by Henry VIII. The grant consisted of £20,000 for the *whole country*. Ludicrously small as it was, it no doubt encouraged the growth of more schools. The Victoria Infant School was opened in 1838, and two more schools were opened by the British and Foreign School Society in 1840 and 1841, one in Mint Lane, another in Newland. About the same time the Wesleyan Sunday Schools were opened in Grantham Street as Day Schools. Others followed at intervals during the century, but the supply of schools was utterly inadequate for the needs of the growing population. In 1870 an Act was passed permitting local School Boards to be elected, which would levy a rate for educational purposes, but Lincoln did not like the idea of paying rates for education and the church wished to maintain its control of the schools. Lincoln preferred to rely upon private subscriptions and the fees of the children to supplement state grants, and so no board was appointed. In 1880 education was made compulsory, and in 1891 it became free, and the schools of Lincoln had to rely on church funds and government grants alone. In 1903 the City Education Authority was brought into existence under the Education Act of 1902, and Lincoln had to have an education rate whether it liked it or not. Lincoln was one of the seven towns in England which up to this date had been content to let the education of its children suffer rather than spend money out of the rates. But the handicap under which modern education suffered in Lincoln has been, in recent years, magnificently overcome, and the city may now be proud of its educational services.

Secondary education had no such difficulties to contend with. The Grammar School not merely kept its endowments at the Reformation, but in Edward VI's reign it received additional endowments and a grant from the Corporation. Except for the payment of sixpence per scholar to the usher and twelve pence to the schoolmaster, it was free. Thus secondary education was advanced while elementary education was abolished! But the Grammar School taught only Latin and Greek, and possibly a little mathematics, so it was no use to the poor who had no means of learning to read and write. Only those who were in "good learning" and able to start on the study of Latin were admitted. The Grammar School was already a very old foundation. It had been established a short time after the founding of the cathedral in 1090 in order to teach the choristers to sing. They also had to learn Grammar, i.e., to write and speak Latin, with the result that the school became divided into two parts, a Choristers' School and a Grammar School. Gradually the Choristers' School became separated from the Grammar School, so that there were now two "secondary schools" in Lincoln with two masters each, whose salaries were provided by endowments. There was also in the twelfth century a very good school belonging to the Jewish community to which the boys of Christian parents who wanted their children to have the best possible education, were sent. In addition there were several chantry priests, as we mentioned above, who no doubt, did a certain amount of elementary teaching, and a number of religious houses, but the educational work accomplished by the friaries and monasteries was probably negligible. At any rate it seems safe to say that there was better provision for education in the time of Grosseteste than in the time of John Hannah five centuries later. After the Reformation the Grammar School was reunited to the Choristers' School and installed in the former Grey Friars' building by the gift of Robert Monson. It was re-endowed, as we have seen and made free for those who wished to study Latin. It was to be inspected twice a year by the dean and mayor. The faults of the schoolmaster were

The Lower Room in the House of the Grey Friars

to be dealt with by the dean, those of the usher by the mayor. In 1624 the Corporation even agreed to buy the books required by "sundry children of poor inhabitants, who for want of books are much hindered in their learning," which shows that the poor were not entirely excluded. A century and a half passes by, a hundred and fifty years of Latin grammar and a little Greek, and then we come to an interesting change. In 1766 the schoolmaster was provided with globes and maps so that he might teach geography. But a curriculum consisting of Latin, Greek and geography did not prove sufficiently attractive, and the school began to decline. In 1850, however, it awoke to new life. The curriculum was now made to include many new subjects—French, mathematics, English Literature, history, "and such other arts and sciences as might be agreed upon." It also ceased to be free. It grew rapidly, both in numbers and in the scope and variety of its work. In 1871 the school was divided into upper and lower schools. In 1884 the upper school moved to new buildings on Lindum Terrace, where the school was reunited in 1900.

In 1906 still larger buildings were erected on Wragby Road, and these were enlarged between 1919 and 1921, and again in 1936.

The Lincoln Girls' High School was built in 1893, and a new Girls' High School on South Park in 1938.

The funds for building the new Grammar School on Lindum Terrace, and for establishing the Lincoln Girls' High School came partly from the endowments of the Lincoln Bluecoat School. In 1602, Richard Smith, a doctor who had lived near Christ's Hospital in London for many years, left money to found a similar institution in Lincoln. After some delay this was done and a house in St. Michael's churchyard became the first Lincoln Bluecoat School. Here 12 boys were educated and maintained until they were apprenticed. The school flourished and the number of boys was greatly increased. A new building was provided in 1785, part of which was afterwards used as the Leeke School. In 1883, the Charity Commissioners decided to close the school on the grounds that elementary education was fully provided for elsewhere in the city, and the funds of the school would be put to better use in

In 1974, Lincoln School and Lincoln Girls' High School will come together on the site of Lincoln School with new buildings added and be known as Lincoln Christ's Hospital School.

providing secondary education. Many interesting relics from the Bluecoat School are preserved in the Museum.

Chancellor Benson and his successor Chancellor Leeke were interested in providing educational opportunities in the city. They organised night classes at the Westgate Club and Robey's Mess Rooms. Later on Chancellor Leeke established a day school in the old Bluecoat School buildings. In 1895 the upper section of the school was moved to the buildings on Monks Road, where the School of Art and evening classes in Science were already established. In the next year, 1896, the connection with the Church House was severed, and the Science Day School came into existence. In 1901 it was renamed "The City of Lincoln Municipal Technical School," and in 1928 it became " The City School."

Leeke School is now the Lincoln College of Art.

The City School, Monks Road moved to new premises on Skelling-thorpe Road in 1968.

Chapter XIX

SOCIAL PROBLEMS.

The Poor Law.

The Reformation had brought great changes in the life of the people of England, and their effects were very evident in Lincoln. In the first place the monasteries and other religious houses had gone, and their inmates dispersed, and with them, of course, the charities which they dispensed to the poor. Certain individuals such as John Broxholme and John Bellow who bought up the monastic lands would benefit, especially as the price of land was rapidly rising owing to the general increase in prices—but no one else. Besides the monasteries, other institutions had disappeared. The religious gilds, as we have seen in an earlier chapter, were attacked and most of them destroyed; but more important even than these in the lives of the common people were the chantries and chantry priests. Forty chantry priests belonging to the Cathedral were granted pensions when the chantries were dissolved, and there may have been others of whom we know nothing. As we have seen, the chantries were the elementary schools of those days, and when they went it was exceedingly difficult to fill their places. What did the common people gain to set against this loss ? It is very difficult to say. They saw their priests harried, and sometimes executed, as we know. They saw some of the local gentry and a number of strangers, mainly tradesmen from London, grow rich on the spoils, but for themselves they were glad if they could earn enough to keep them from actual want in this period of rising prices and fluctuating trade.

HIGH STREET
(From a painting by A. C. Pugin, 1762-1832)

THE BEGINNING OF THE POOR LAW.

Times were hard in the period of the Reformation. In 1546 it was necessary to legalise begging in Lincoln :—" Such poor people in every parish as are not able to work to get their living, to have signs given them with which to ask alms weekly, and none to give any alms but to such as have these signs." There was unemployment, too. In 1562 it was ordered that unemployed workmen and labourers should stand with their tools for at least an hour every day at the Stonebow in order that those who needed workmen might find them. The effect of the Dissolution was still being felt. In 1571 it was stated that the county had been very largely cleared of "timber, wood, coal, thatch, turf and other necessaries by many greedy persons, owners of the same since the dissolution of the late religious houses, to the great decay of the poor ancient City of Lincoln."

Some method had to be devised for giving relief to the poor. In 1557 there were collections for those who were stricken with the plague, but it was no use leaving such a serious problem to the whims and caprices of town councils. The state itself began to interfere and in 1572 a compulsory rate was ordered to be levied by Act of Parliament. New officers were to be elected as Collectors, or Overseers of the Poor, in every parish, and they were to see to it that a stock of materials was kept, so that those who wanted work but could not find it might be employed, while the sick, the old, and the infant poor were to be relieved according to their needs. There was one other category of poor who had to be kept in mind ; those who had learned to live by their wits—by begging and thieving —those who, like Autolycus, snatched the washing from the hedges, or better still, a well lined purse from a farmer's hand as he jogged home from market. These were the rogues and vagabonds— thousands of them—who haunted the roads and lanes and camped out on the common in the reign of Good Queen Bess. Sometimes they joined together in bands and terrified whole villages, and people began to sing " Hark ! Hark ! the Dogs do Bark, the beggars are coming to town." Some of them had been farmers who had lost their farms owing to the enclosure movement and the growth of large farms at the expense of small ones, and others were unemployed owing to gild regulations or to the ups and downs of trade following upon the wars that were taking place on the Continent. In 1576 a new remedy was tried. Sturdy vagabonds were first to be put in the stocks and whipped and then sent to a kind of workhouse-prison, the House of Correction, as it was called, where they were to be made to work.

In 1612 the mayor and council of Lincoln decided to use the lower room of the Grey Friars building for this purpose, and in 1615 a " Jersey School " was established here in which the poor were employed on spinning with Jersey spinning wheels and on knitting. It continued to be used for this purpose until about 1830.

But besides the Jersey School the individual parishes tried to find employment for the poor. This was one of the duties of the Overseers and Churchwardens, and they continued to carry it out for many years. In 1746 we find the parish officers of St. Peter in Eastgate buying flax and setting the poor to spin and weave it in return for wages. That is the way they tried to solve the unemployment problem in those days.

They did a great many other things besides. They apprenticed poor children to masters and fitted them out with clothes—gowns, aprons, stockings, etc., in the case of a girl ; shirts, shoes, a hat, and a pair of " Briches " for a boy. They sent bread and ale to sick persons and even provided a nurse for them. They gave allowances to poor people—4s. per week per family—who were unable to work, and one of their regular paupers, Mary Heal, they successfully married off, and so transferred the burden to someone else. They paid for her wedding and gave her a dowry, too, which cost the parish £4 altogether, but it was probably worth it. They also recommended treatment for the poor when they were ill. Robert Norman, for instance, was taken by another pauper, Sammy Wood, to be dipped in the Cold Bath on the south side of Sewell Road. It killed him, but perhaps they found this worth it, too !

In the second half of the eighteenth century they seem to have grown more mean. They tried to pack off their poor to a work-house kept by a private contractor who charged three shillings a week each and presumably made a profit out of them. He charged extra for burial expenses. No doubt they were high. We also find the Overseers going to a great deal of trouble to turn out poor strangers who belonged to other towns. They turned out the Spencer family in this way, first to York and then to Horncastle. It cost them £9 8s. to do it, which would have kept the Spencers a long time at 4s. a week, but the Churchwarden at the time was a woman, Mrs. Mompesson, and she would have none of them. In this way, the poor were looked after by the different parishes, as we see from the books which the parish officers left behind, until the great Act of 1834 united the parishes into Poor Law Unions, and in 1837 the Lincoln Union Workhouse was erected which provided accom-modation for the poor of ninety-nine parishes. Then the poor were made, if it was possible, more miserable than ever.

HIGHWAYS.

Another problem which the parishes had to face was the mainten-ance of the roads. Under an act of Philip and Mary in 1555, each parish had to appoint Surveyors or Overseers of the Highway for this purpose, and in this same parish, St. Peter in Eastgate, we read

The Lincoln Workhouse was demolished in 1965 and the site is now used for Council housing.

of them arranging for the roads of the parish to be cleaned and for five lamps to be bought, set up, and lighted. They also saw that the rubbish from the ruined churches was cleared out and carted on to the roads, and they had the duty of keeping the parish well in repair ; not such an easy task as it sounds, apparently, for the bucket was continually falling in and having to be fished out again, and not only the bucket, but a " Dogg," then a " Catt," and finally a " pige." It cost sixpence to get the pig out, but the cat could not be found.

LAW AND ORDER.

Besides the Overseers of the Poor and the Surveyors of the Highway, there were armed watchmen to keep guard throughout the night and also the parish constable. The usual punishment for wrong doers was the stocks and the whipping post. In January 1560 the city council decided that two pairs of stocks should be made, one for the south ward and one for the north. There was also a cuck-stool for ducking women who were accused of brawling or " scolding," and it remained in use until the end of the seventeenth century, for in 1685, a new one had to be provided at a cost of 55s. 8d. Surprising as it may be, certain types of prisoners continued to be branded with a hot iron until the same period, as the following entry in the city accounts for 1699 shows :—" For an engine for burning prisoners in the cheek 10s." In addition to stocks and a cuck-stool there was a pillory. It was in existence in 1202 when a stranger who had been placed in it " let his feet drop " and was strangled before anyone could help him. In the fourteenth century John de Graingham, who had stolen three hens and a cock of the value of 8d., was placed in it. We hear of it again in 1520, when a man was sentenced to be set in the pillory and to have his ears nailed to it, and it was still in use three centuries later when John Horton was ordered to stand in the pillory .on the Cornhill for one hour in 1803, and Martin Dowdell, a man who had been found guilty of perjury, was ordered to the pillory on Castle Hill for one hour, on 21st March, 1817.

PRISONS.

In addition to all these there were the prisons. The oldest prison in Lincoln, as you might expect, is the castle, and in Cob Hall we may still see the drawing of a stag-hunt carved on the wall by a prisoner who had probably been brought in from the county. For centuries prisoners were cast into dungeons in the castle buildings. Some of these had no windows and the only means of ventilation was by way of an iron grating. One of them, called " The Witch Hole," was used as a prison for the Royalist, William Caldwell, of Thurgarton, in the Civil War. " He had no other bed but the ground and no pillow but the hard stones." Another was so small that when four prisoners were in it only one could lie down ; the others had to stand. A more modern prison stood in the castle yard when the great prison reformer, John Howard, visited it in 1788. There were forty-nine prisoners locked up in it, of whom twenty were debtors and twenty-nine were felons.

Largely as a result of John Howard's efforts a new prison was being built in 1788. The debtors were separated from the felons, and their accommodation depended upon the amount they could pay. A debtor had to pay for his board and lodging in prison in those days. One wonders how this helped him to pay his debts. For 2s. 6d. a week he could have a bed to himself; for 1s. 6d. he had to share it with another. There was a good supply of hard and soft water, and all the felons had straw for their beds, and three blankets and a rug to cover them—truly " an excellent gaol," in the words of a writer in 1812.

But the castle was a county gaol, and the city had a gaol of its own in the Stonebow. It was here that the city courts were held, and the eastern wing of the building was used as a prison. A narrow lane, now widened to form Saltergate, ran alongside and a grated window in the prison wall enabled prisoners to talk to passers-by. Two upper rooms were used for debtors. The felons were kept in two dungeons with damp earth floors. There was no court in which they might exercise, no water supply, no straw ; yet when they were released they had to pay 6s. 8d. as a fee to the gaoler ! Their only relaxation was provided by the iron grating overlooking this lane, which enabled them to talk with their friends and also to receive presents of food and drink—especially drink. A visitor in 1802 said the prisoners were half starved, half suffocated, and in a state of continual intoxication. The prison was one of the worst in the kingdom, a disgrace to the city, and shocking to humanity.

In 1809 the inmates were transferred to a new prison that had just been completed near Clasketgate (The Sessions House), and it was used until 1878 when the prison on Greetwell Road was opened.

CHAPTER XX.

THE COMING OF DEMOCRACY.

It is clear from what we have said that the parish officers were very important people. They looked after the poor, repaired the roads, arrested vagrants and kept the peace. But over the parishes stood the corporation. It was responsible for trying the offenders whom the parish constable caught—and for the dreadful gaols to which they were sent. Its members also looked after the common pastures and arable fields that surrounded the city, and in the name of the freemen of Lincoln they administered the city property, land, houses and the navigation of the Fossdyke. The corporation was, therefore, an important body. It was very different from the modern corporation, of course. It did not supply gas, electricity and transport. It did not look after the poor. It never dreamed of educating the people of Lincoln, but it had great powers of good and ill in its hands, and it is important to know how they were used.

In the very early days, before the rise of the corporation, men had managed their affairs through the local courts. They collected together as freemen had the right to do, to declare the law and also to carry it out. They saw to it themselves. The system was in many ways democratic in that every freeman was expected to take an active part according to his grade in society.

We should remember there were a great many local courts in those days—the Shire Courts, the Hundred Courts, the Manor Courts and the courts of the king at Westminster. In all except the last the people themselves were the judges, under the leadership, no doubt, of the more wealthy and powerful among them. They knew the local law and no one else did, and they solemnly declared it according to the forms and ceremonies that their fathers and forefathers had used. This was true even of the greatest local court of all, the Shire Court. The sheriff presided, it is true, but it was the freeholders of the shire who made the decisions. The sheriff merely carried them out.

The only person who could overrule the local courts in a city like Lincoln was the king, and as time passed even the king's power over the city ceased to be exercised, and in practice it became free. The mayor, sheriffs, citizens and commonalty were themselves the lord of the manor. This came about gradually in the fourteenth century and we hear no more of the king suddenly levying taxes or tallages in addition to the regular " farm " of the city. (Henry III on one occasion had taxed the city to the tune of £1,000). Nor do we hear again of the king taking away the city's privilege of self-government. He threatens to do so from time to time, but he never carries out his threats.

Thus the city became more and more free, but did it become more and more democratic ? On the contrary, the people gradually lost whatever democratic control they ever had, and the city came to be ruled by a small clique of well-to-do traders, merchants and landowners.

There were complaints from " the commonalty " in Henry III's reign. For instance, they had always enjoyed the right of meeting every Monday in the Borough Court, where they helped the city magistrates to carry out the law, but in Henry III's reign we find them complaining bitterly that the court no longer met regularly, and asking that their old rights shall be restored. This is interesting.

It looks as though the ordinary citizen was losing what little say he ever had in the affairs of the city, for if the Borough Court—the folk moot—is not held, how can he make his voice heard? At this time, as we know, there were many quarrels between the rich, who controlled the city, and the main body of citizens. The rich could even increase the annual charges upon the town without consulting their fellow citizens. They promised an additional £10 to the lord of Boston Fair, for instance, " without any assent or consent of the commonalty," and turned a deaf ear to their complaints. They robbed and oppressed the poor citizens in other ways, as we have seen, and in 1290 the quarrels between the ruling class and the "commonalty" gave rise to such disorder that the king had to interfere. He took the government of the city into his own hands and ruled it through his own officers.

New regulations were drawn up for the management of the city affairs, but the quarrels continued. In 1325 it was complained that " the Great Lords " themselves paid nothing. The " mean people " were taxed at will without their consent. They alone were forced to keep the nightly watches. The taxes which they paid to keep up the wall of the city were pocketed by the rich for their own purposes, and no accounts were rendered to the people. They appealed to the king himself to help them, but they obtained no redress.

They were particularly bitter because they were allowed no share in the election of the mayor and bailiffs, and they were supported in their claim by the dean and chapter of the cathedral—which only made matters worse, for the jealousy between the magnates of the city and the dignitaries of the church was intense. In 1393 the commonalty appealed to the king again, but without result, and they were gradually excluded from any share at all in civic affairs.

They not merely took no part in the election of their rulers, but they also lost what is called their right of "veto," *i.e.*, their right to forbid the mayor and his friends to do something which they disliked. Formerly all important decisions had been submitted to the citizens in common counsel, which enabled them to exercise, if they wished, their right of "veto," but by the fifteenth century this right was entirely lost. It is true the mayor had to obtain the consent of fifty or sixty citizens to any motion advanced by him "for the good of the city," but by 1511 it was sufficient if twenty-four discreet and honest persons, together with the twelve aldermen should agree. How the "twenty-four discreet and honest" ones were chosen we do not know, but not by the commonalty we may be sure.

In opposition to the group of rich men who ruled the city, there grew up about 1350 a gild of the "common and middling folk," and they did their best to exclude from membership anyone "of rank of mayor or bailiffs," and they made a rule that if any such person insisted on joining them, they should neither meddle with the business of the gild, nor be appointed officers. Thus one monopoly, as so often happens, called forth another. But though the richer citizens had managed to get the power into their own hands, we must not imagine they were entirely happy or at peace. On the contrary, they quarrelled continuously. Aldermen were sometimes removed from the bench, and attempts were made to upset the election of the mayor.

In 1628, soon after Charles I came to the throne, a new charter was granted to the city, and from it we learn exactly how the city was governed. First of all there was the mayor, who was chosen from the aldermen by the common council for a year. But what was the common council ? It was a body of forty-five citizens who sat for life. When a vacancy occurred, the mayor and the senior aldermen (those who had been mayors) drew up a list of the names of persons who had served the offices of sheriff or chamberlain—usually the three seniors who were eligible—and the common council voted upon them, and usually chose the first, that is the senior ex-sheriff or chamberlain. Thus the only way to get on the governing body of the town was to serve in one of these offices. But how were the sheriffs and chamberlains chosen ? There were two sheriffs, of whom the mayor chose one, and the common council the other. There were four chamberlains, and the mayor chose them all from among his own personal friends. All semblance of popular election had vanished.

The office of mayor was, therefore, very important, but only aldermen were eligible for it. Who were the aldermen ? They first appear in 1300 when certain " Provisions" were drawn up for the better government of the city. They were described as twelve discreet men who were to act with the mayor as magistrates, but we are not told how they were chosen. Probably they were elected in some way ; at least, it is likely that their names were submitted to the "commonalty in common counsel." But this right was not mentioned in the charter of 1628. Here we learn that the aldermen were elected for life by the common council from among themselves. When a vacancy occurred, the mayor and aldermen drew up a list of three names from amongst the members of the common council, and the common councilmen chose one by secret ballot.

The mayor and aldermen, chosen in this way, were the real governors of the city, and they ruled it, with two short interruptions, for more than two hundred years.

We might ask at this point—where did the mayor and council meet ? At first they met in the hall of the Merchants' Gild. The

The Close Gatehouse which stood at the western end of Eastgate
(Demolished early in the nineteenth century)

reason for this was, no doubt, that the leading merchants were also among the rulers of the city. Gradually the Merchant Gild disappeared. Its work was taken over by craft gilds, and especially by the mayor and corporation, but its hall remained the headquarters of the city government. Exactly where the first Guildhall was we

cannot say, but we know that in 1237 it was handed over to the
Grey Friars, and the mayor and corporation were provided with new
premises. These were situated over the arch which stood on the
site of the present Stonebow. Here some of the aldermen sat as a
a court of justice and heard the pleas of the city. Here the
" Clothing," as the whole council was called, gathered to elect the
chamberlains and sheriffs, and it was here that the mayor, in order
to celebrate his elevation to the highest office in the city, entertained
the " Clothing " to a banquet. We have no menu cards of those happy
occasions, but we know that the tenants of the corporation had to
include among their rents such items as " one good fat crammed
turkey," " a couple of fat crammed capons," " one dozen good sweet
pigeons," " one pound of refined sugar." These rents were payable
on September 26th, *i.e.*, at the time of the annual mayormaking.
There were other occasions for more modest junketings. On
St. Thomas's Day the mayor and the governors, masters and boys of
the Bluecoat School, took a lunch together consisting of buns and
spiced ale, and afterwards attended divine service in St. Mark's.

Let us see how the affairs of the city were managed under the
government we have described. As we have seen, the citizens at
large had no control of it, yet they had to accept its decisions, and
if they objected, or defied the corporation, they would be brought
up and tried by the very men against whom they were protesting.
For we should remember, the senior aldermen—those who had
been mayors—were also magistrates. The law which they helped
to make, they also carried out. But, you will say, there was also
the king's court as well as the local court. There were the Assizes
presided over by a royal judge, as well as Quarter Sessions presided
over by the mayor or recorder, and there was one further safeguard ;
there was the Grand Jury, without which nothing could be done in
either of these courts. If a road had to be mended at the city's

expense, or a criminal hanged at the city gaol, it was the Grand Jury that first " sat on " the case. Was this not sufficient ? Perhaps so, but we should remember that the Grand Jury consisted of chamberlains and ex-chamberlains only, and chamberlains, as we have seen, were chosen from the mayor's personal friends. The influence of the mayor and the ruling group was felt in all branches of the city government.

Let us consider for a moment from what part of the community they were drawn. In order to do so we must distinguish between the freemen and non-freemen, since freemen only were eligible for office of any kind. The differences between them were very wide. Only the freemen had any claim at all to the duties and privileges of citizens. It was from them that the mayor chose the chamberlains, and the common council chose the sheriffs. Yet four-fifths of the city rates were paid by non-freemen, while half the freemen lived outside the city and therefore paid no rates at all ! Such was the position in 1835, when the Government caused an enquiry to be made into the way in which the cities and boroughs of England were being governed. The Report tells us that there were 603 freemen of Lincoln at this time, of whom 300 only lived in the city and governed it. The remaining 10,000 inhabitants had no part or lot in its affairs. The freemen were a tiny minority of privileged persons.

Who were they and how did they come by their privileges ? Originally many of them were members of the craft gilds, but not all craftsmen were freemen. For some reason the fullers and the dyers were deliberately excluded from the privilege of citizenship, although they contributed along with the other gilds to the rates and taxes, but all other gildsmen ranked as " free citizens."

There were no doubt many others, besides the members of craft gilds, who were " free citizens "—landowners in the city, and merchants, for instance, who paid the city rates and taxes, and others upon whom the city fathers conferred rights of citizenship as a special honour or in return for payment, and of course the privileges of citizenship would be handed down from father to son. Thus it was possible to become a freeman of the city of Lincoln in several different ways, but the members of the craft gilds predominated.

That does not mean that they necessarily worked at their craft ; many members of craft gilds were tradesmen who had exchanged the workshop for the counter. Thus the gilds, like the city itself, tended to become divided into two groups, one consisting of tradesmen and merchants, the other of men who, after serving their apprenticeship, set up as small masters and claimed the " freedom of the city."

As we have seen it was only the rich freemen who had any real power. The rest, in spite of being free citizens, had no say in the city's affairs, but they had certain advantages over the non-freemen. They had their own commons. The Holmes Common, acquired as the land was drained, and Monks' Leys, acquired after the dissolution of the monasteries, were kept for their exclusive use. The remaining commons—West Common, South Common, Cowpaddle and Swine Green—were pastured by householders, including the freemen. They also had an advantage over non-freemen with regard to the leasing of corporation property and the distribution of charities. The leases had been taken out many years earlier, when the rents were very low, and in spite of increasing prices, the rents remained the same. Thus the revenue of the corporation did not rise with the rising value of the land, and in order to meet their increasing costs, they levied taxation upon all. Non-freemen were being taxed for the benefit of the freemen ! No wonder non-freemen were sometimes willing to pay from £100 to £500 to obtain the privileges of burgess right !

There was one privilege upon which freemen set an especially high value. This was the right to vote for members of parliament. Only freemen had this right and they made good use of it. The candidates who asked for their support adopted different methods from those with which we are familiar today. They bought the voters coals. They gave them drinks. They paid the expenses of young men who wished to obtain their freedom, and the more fiercely the contest was fought, the better it was for the freemen of Lincoln with votes to sell.

In the early part of the nineteenth century it was found that half the freemen lived outside Lincoln, many of them in London, but they had the vote, and of the other half that lived in Lincoln only a small proportion, consisting of fifty or sixty persons, exercised any real power.

Under such conditions there was great temptation to abuse their position, and it is not surprising that they came to look upon the city and its revenues as their private property. Indeed, it is remarkable that complaints were so few. Whether this is due to the honesty and efficiency of the ruling families, or to the feeling that complaint was hopeless in face of the corporation's power, it is difficult to say.

The influence which wealth gave is well brought out by the history of the Ellison family. In 1741 Richard Ellison, who later became a banker, acquired a lease of the Fossdyke tolls from the corporation, at the annual charge, it is said, of £75 a year. He brought about numerous improvements in the navigation and a large increase of trade took place. But his successors neglected to continue his good work, and no further improvements in the important waterway were made. This was a serious matter in view of the steadily increasing volume of trade, and many bitter complaints were made. But nothing was done. A later Ellison continued to draw the revenues, which rose to the enormous figure of £12,000 a year, and to pay the stipulated £75 to the corporation, but to all suggestions that he should improve the waterway he turned a deaf ear. He even ignored the urgent notice sent to him by the corporation on the matter. The corporation grumbled, but he did nothing. Why not? Partly because he was an important and prominent man—Member of Parliament for the City, Recorder, Chairman of the Court of Quarter Sessions and Colonel of the City Cavalry. But more than this; he was also part owner of Smith Ellison's Bank, where the corporation kept its accounts. Members of the corporation kept their private accounts there also, and the accounts both of the corporation and of its members were not infrequently overdrawn. While the corporation might have braved the Colonel of the City Cavalry, it dared not defy a partner in Smith Ellison's Bank, especially as the Town Clerk, who would have had to carry the challenge, was his nominee !

Under these conditions, the word " democracy " must have sounded sweet in the ears of Lincoln citizens, and during the period of the French Revolution and the subsequent disturbances it was frequently heard. After the Reform Act of 1832 had shown that political reform could no longer be delayed, the government of Lincoln and other cities was completely overhauled. In place of the " close corporation " of fifty or sixty persons, the government of the city was thrown open by the Municipal Corporation Act (1835) to all who paid rates. No doubt the rich citizens continued to play the leading part, for they alone had both the knowledge and the leisure to undertake the work of local government, but the smaller tradesmen also began to take part in the affairs of the city, and even the poor, if they paid rates, had the vote.

The new city council was composed of earnest reformers, who thought that the insignia, robes and plate of the old corporation were remnants of municipal corruption. They decided to sell the civic plate, which included a two-handled vase cup holding nearly a gallon, silver coffee and tea pots, forks and spoons and many other articles. These were accordingly sold in April, 1836, for a total sum of £240.

Fortunately all proposals to sell the maces and swords were defeated, and these with other interesting reminders of the past are still preserved, and, after being neglected for a time, now serve their proper purpose in civic ceremonies.

THE BAIL.

As soon as the city began to grow free and independent it found itself in conflict with the Bail. Here the constable of the castle ruled as a military governor, not only over his garrison of soldiers, but also over the householders who lived in the outer bailey of the castle—the Bail, as it was called. They were citizens of the borough. They paid taxes with other citizens and went to the borough court. But the constable also had a court. It was held every Tuesday at the castle gate, and in addition the constable claimed the right of testing weights and measures and supervising the quality of bread and ale. Now all these rights were very profitable, since offenders were usually punished by means of a fine, and disputes between the city and the constable were bound to arise. The bailiffs in the city, as we have seen in an earlier section, had to raise their annual payment to the king—the city " farm." Should we be surprised that they cast envious eyes on the profits which the constable was drawing from the citizens in the Bail, or that they tried to prove that in certain kinds of disputes, *e.g.*, disputes about land, markets, tolls, weights and measures, citizens, whether of the Bail or not, must resort to the borough court and no other ? Then there were disputes over the chattels of felons or fugitives, the holding of hirings of reapers or servants, and the rents from stalls in the Bail. The Bail, the bailiffs said, was part of the city, and a very large part, being a third of the whole, and its inhabitants ought to contribute to the city taxes like other citizens. Moreover servants and reapers preferred to be hired in the Bail because city officers were prevented by the constable from chastising them, with the result that the price of labour had gone up.

The constable of the castle at this time (1375–90) was Oliver de Barton, and he was holding it on behalf of John of Gaunt, Duke of Lancaster, and in 1390 the Duke brought an action against the mayor and four ex-mayors for interfering with the affairs of the Bail. They had prevented merchants from setting up their stalls, it was said, and they had compelled residents of the Bail to come to the city courts for the testing of bread and ale, which ought to be done in the Duke's court. They had built houses in the dykes of the castle and drawn rents from them, although they were on the Duke's ground.

And so it went on, generation after generation for centuries, from Henry III to Henry VIII, and even in Elizabeth's reign, and it was not until 1845 that the Bail was finally united with the city. But it still had its own Court Leet, at which inhabitants had to attend and answer to their names, or pay twopence. It had its own town crier and supervised its own weights and measures. Thus did the old feudal divisions of Lincoln linger on, into times of living memory.

The city authorities set up stones on each side of the roads leading through the gateways of the upper Roman city, the walls of which marked the original boundaries of the Bail. These stones, which stood on the city side of the moat outside the walls, marked the limits of the areas ruled by the constable of the castle, the dean and chapter, and the mayor and city council. We can still see these stones on Steep Hill, in Eastgate, and in Newport.

THE CLOSE.

One other ancient division lingered still longer, and to some extent is with us today. This was the Close, or enclosure surrounding the cathedral. It dates from the reign of William the Conqueror, when Remigius, the first Norman bishop, removed the See of Dorchester to Lincoln. A site was found for the new cathedral in the south-eastern quarter of the Bail, and the clergy who were to serve it were established in the same district, not merely because it was more convenient, but also because it was safer. The cathedral of Remigius was something more than a very large church. It was also a very strong fortress, a place of refuge against the conquered English and possible bands of roving Danes.

A large body of clergy, their servants and retainers were established in houses at the foot of the great building, and the question arose of the responsibility for keeping the peace among them and raising taxes. Disputes were bound to arise with the city over the question and in a letter sent to the city authorities by Henry II, we learn

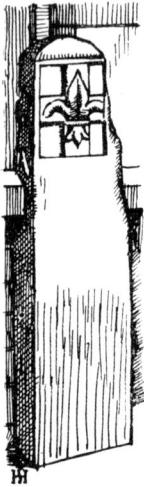

Boundary Stone between the Bail and City

Boundary stones have now gone from Eastgate.

that the dean and chapter were allowed to hold a weekly court, called the Galilee Court, for every kind of dispute affecting the inhabitants of the Close. They were entirely free from interference, either by the city or the castle, and were an independent community of their own, and in order to make this fact as plain as possible, they built a twelve-foot wall around themselves, and lived within it.

The East Gate of the Close which stood in Eastgate near the Deanery
Demolished early in the nineteenth century

Permission to do this was given to the dean and chapter in 1285, shortly after Bishop Sutton had entertained Edward I at Nettleham. The king's licence is still preserved in the cathedral library. In 1318 Edward II allowed the wall to be raised and fortified. The work was completed by 1329.

These precautions were necessary, we are told, on account of the murders and outrages committed in the streets and lanes around the precincts !

From this we gather that the relations between the city and the cathedral were not entirely happy. Indeed, they were marked by long and furious quarrels. The chief causes of dispute were the profits arising from market tolls. Ought the dean and chapter to be allowed to set up stalls for the sale of merchandise in the Close and collect the tolls for the use of the cathedral ? If so, they ought to contribute to the city taxes, which, of course, the dean and chapter refused to do.

And so the mayor and other citizens flew to arms, and tried to prevent the merchants from setting up stalls in the Close by force, and even threatened to kill the merchants if the dean and chapter continued to hold their market. This brought the king into the quarrel. In 1390 he commanded the city, under heavy penalties, to keep the peace, and—since the dean and chapter were unable to get justice done to them, because the citizens would not bear witness against one another in the law courts, but on the contrary, would cheerfully swear false oaths to disprove the allegations of the dean and chapter—in future, whenever such complaints should arise, the case should be tried, not in Lincoln before Lincoln juries, but in the Court of King's Bench in London, before juries drawn from outside the city !

But disturbances continued. Men who were charged with crime in the city fled to the Close to escape arrest. Mayors and bailiffs sometimes fled to the Close rather than serve their terms of office, and the dean and chapter supported the commonalty against the rich merchants who, as we have seen, were oppressing them, especially after the Black Death. Who were the fugitives who fled

to the Close for refuge from the city magistrates ?   Some of them
were leaders of the poor in their quarrel with the rich, and the city
authorities were roused to fury when their enemies escaped them
by fleeing to the Close.   During the Christmas of 1393, several
clerks and ministers were maimed in the quarrels arising from
these causes.   The services were interrupted.   The church, the

The Old Registry (North Side)
Demolished in 1815

cemetery and the city itself were so polluted that it was impossible to complete the Christmas celebrations.

There is no reason to think that the dean and chapter shed their blood in this quarrel because they had any special love for the commonalty. Rather it was due to their hatred of the city rulers who attacked their privileges and seized their revenues. When we remember the dean and chapter contributed nothing to the city taxes, while at the same time they harboured the criminals as well as the agitators of the city, we can see that there was good cause for bitterness.

But as the wealth of the city declined in the fifteenth century, and numbers of both rich and poor citizens left it to trade in more populous places, the quarrels with the dean and chapter ceased, and a close understanding began to take the place of the old enmity. Since there were far fewer merchants to set up their stalls, there was less to quarrel about, and so the dean and chapter had no interest in harbouring agitators or criminals from the city. Indeed, so friendly were the relations between the city and Close that the mayor of the city in 1520 and '21 was made clerk of the chapter in 1522! He is not the only important official of the chapter to serve the highest offices of the city. Perhaps the supply of rich merchants was declining and it may have been difficult to get that kind of citizen to fill the city offices. Some citizens disliked this new-fangled harmony which gave such power to the old rivals of the city. " It was never a good world," they said, " since the bishop had a hand in choosing the mayor. It would be as well for him and the dean if they kept out of it. Should they come to the Hall during the election they might be cast out of the window, and then, at least, they would know the worst ! "

But though there were no more quarrels, the special privileges of the Close remained until the nineteenth century.

The Reform Bill brought the Close and Bail into the city parliamentary constituency, and in 1845 the revising barristers under the Municipal Corporations Act of 1835 brought them into the municipality also. Then they lost the separate existence which they had enjoyed for many centuries.

BEAUMONT FEE.

There was one other district in Lincoln which was not governed by the city authorities during the middle ages. The Danish town, as we have seen, contained a number of divisions, each ruled by one of the most powerful citizens.

Only one of these areas appears to have survived the Norman Conquest as an independent unit. This was the manor of Hungate. Soon after the Conquest it probably belonged to Alfred of Lincoln. From him it seems to have passed to Alan of Lincoln, and then to Ralph Bayeux, who married Alan's daughter.

The Bayeux family held many manors within reach of the city, and they made the manor of Hungate the centre from which they controlled their estates in this part of England. A court was set up here, which the tenants of their other lands were bound to attend. If they failed to appear they were fined.

Edward II granted the manor of Hungate, with other lands, to his favourite, Isabella de Vesci, and later to her brother Henry de Beaumont. The ancient manor house probably stood a little to the south of West Parade, on the site of the building now used as the offices of the Public Health Department. It became known as " Vesci Hall," and the manor as " The Liberty of Beaumont Fee." A " fee " is a piece of land.

The Beaumonts lost the estates during the Wars of the Roses and in 1514 they were given to Lord Howard, son of the Duke of

Norfolk, in return for his services at Flodden. The Norfolk family sold the manor in 1700. The manor had kept its independence because it belonged to a family which was well able to protect its own interests, but when it passed into feebler hands, the manor was soon broken up among small owners, and lost many of its privileges.

In 1927 the corporation of Lincoln bought the house built by Mr. John Hayward on the site of the old manor house.

During the thirteenth century the baronial court met at intervals of six weeks, and it was held until the early eighteenth century. The mayor of the city and the dean and chapter of the cathedral were among those who should have attended the court, though in later years they usually found it more convenient to pay a small fine for absence. Tenants who neglected waterways or fences, or obstructed roads, were dealt with at this court. The manor had its own bailiff who attended the Assizes, and its own arrangements for dealing with criminals. City constables were not allowed to arrest offenders within the manor and this sometimes caused trouble. Occasionally, debtors took refuge here from their creditors in the Bail, Close or City.

Some of the court rolls have been preserved and they give us a very good idea of the way in which a lord ruled his manor.

CHAPTER XXI.

THE RISE OF MODERN LINCOLN.

The year 1835, as we have seen, marks a turning point in Lincoln's history. It was then that the old corporation was swept away, and a new system of government by men elected by the citizens was introduced, and a little later the old medieval divisions between City and Bail and Close were abolished, and the authority of the people's representatives ruled unchallenged.

What lay behind this great change? Men do not suddenly decide to sweep away old institutions and ways of living and substitute new ones without good reason, and it takes them a very long time to get their minds accustomed to altering things in this way. There must have been some deep seated cause at work, which after many years of silent pressure underneath, suddenly came to the top and changed the *outside* in accordance with the changes which had already taken place *inside*.

Let us, therefore, try to penetrate into the *inside* and see what has been taking place in the long quiet period between the end of the middle ages and the year 1835. By far the most remarkable change we shall notice is in the numbers of the people. From Domesday Book we know roughly how many people lived in Lincoln in the time of William the Conqueror. There were about 6,000, a large number for those days, but by the middle of the fifteenth century, when the city, as we have seen, was no longer the prosperous centre of former days, the population had gone down to less than 2,000. During the sixteenth century it probably climbed a little to about 2,500, and a century later, in 1676, it had reached roughly

3,250, little more than half what it had been in the time of William the Conqueror! But in 1831, when the first careful census of the town was taken, the number had risen to no fewer than 11,217.

What had happened to bring about this remarkable change? Was it due to the rise of new industries which called for child labour, or the poor law, which gave an allowance according to the size of the family? Both these explanations are often advanced to account for the rise of population at this time, but both are very unsatisfactory, if not entirely wrong. A much more satisfactory reason is that there was more and better food than ever before, and therefore people—especially babies—had a better chance of survival. For the first time in history it was possible to get a supply of fresh meat and fresh milk *all the year round*! Previously the only kind of meat available in winter time was salted carcases (unless you had a dovecote and kept pigeons) and there was practically no milk at all. Such cows and goats as were kept for breeding were, as farmers say, " dried off " in the winter. One cannot help wondering how parents ever brought up their babies under such conditions. As a matter of fact, a very large number were not brought up at all, since more than half of those born died in infancy.

But with the change of diet—fresh meat, fresh milk, and vegetables —all this was changed. Scurvy died out, and rickets was no longer a serious scourge. People began, also, to throw aside their thick woollen clothes and wear the new cheap cotton clothes that were coming in. The result was the death rate declined, and the population rose by leaps and bounds. There were, no doubt, other causes, *e.g.*, hospitals, vaccination and the growth of medical science. In Lincoln a General Hospital was established in 1769 and no doubt it saved many lives. It was particularly useful in enabling doctors to observe the effects of their treatment upon the patients. If they died (as they often did) from a particular course of treatment, another was tried in later cases.

But the chief reason was undoubtedly the revolution in diet from salt carcases to fresh meat. What made the revolution possible? The answer is a very simple, but perhaps unexpected one—the turnip! Owing to the introduction of turnips, and also clover crops in the seventeenth and eighteenth centuries, it was possible to keep all kinds of cattle alive throughout the winter, and a supply of fresh meat and milk became possible all the year round for the first time in the history of England. Which is the more important, King Charles' head or the turnip? We learn a great deal in our history book about King Charles and the unfortunate way in which he lost his head, but how many of us could write the story of the turnip? And yet, but for the turnip, how many of us would be here now?

CHANGES IN AGRICULTURE. ENCLOSURES.

In order to grow turnips, clover, and other " green " crops that were coming in from the seventeenth century, new methods of farming were called for. It was particularly important that farmers should be able to grow *what* they liked and *when* they liked, if these new experiments were to be tried out. But according to the old system, the arable land lay in strips in two or three open fields. Every second or third year, as the case may be, they were fallowed, and grew nothing at all. During the fallow year, every farmer who had common rights could let his sheep and cattle graze over the land, so that it was impossible for any farmer to grow experimental crops on it. Therefore, progressive farmers wished to enclose the land so that they could do as they liked with it. The landlords agreed because they could get more rent when the land was enclosed. The cottagers and small farmers disagreed because it meant that they would lose the use of the common, but no one listened to them, and enclosures went on. The result was that the output of all agricultural produce increased rapidly, and Lincoln began to feel the benefit of the change. Defoe described the city in 1724 as " dead, decayed and dirty," but he was wrong. It may have been decayed, and it was certainly dirty, but it was not dead. On the contrary, it was on the eve of a new lease of life that has lasted until our own time, and shows no sign of coming to an end.

It started with the agricultural changes we have described. Lincoln had always, from Roman times, been the centre of a very rich agricultural district, and after the decay of medieval trade and manufactures, it had to rely almost entirely on agriculture and the industries connected with it. The ruined monasteries and churches, according to Defoe, had been turned into barns, outhouses and stables, and even the hog-styes were built church fashion, with stone walls and arched windows. But a new life was stirring in the country districts. The fens were being drained. The barren heaths were being brought under the plough, and more butter and meat was being produced than ever before. In 1736 the corporation caused a new Butter Market to be built, a sure sign of reviving trade. In 1741 the Fossdyke was taken over by Mr. Richard Ellison and its navigation greatly improved, and in 1774 the old Butchery, or Meat Shambles, in Clasketgate, was rebuilt. About 1846 the markets for beast, sheep and pigs were moved to the fields above Monks' Road. Beast were formerly sold in the Old Beast Square, now part of the Sessions House grounds, sheep in the " Sheep Square," now the site of St. Swithin's Church, and pigs in Unity Square. The Old Corn Exchange was opened in 1848. At no time in the city's history were there so many horses and sheep brought to Lincoln's great fairs. The " dead, decayed and dirty " city of Defoe had begun to revive.

Open Fields and Turnpike Roads

THE ENCLOSURE OF LINCOLN.

The towns as well as the villages had a problem of enclosure to face, but it was complicated by the question of freemen's rights. If the open land was enclosed the freemen must be compensated in some way, and we can well imagine the arguments that were bandied to and fro when the question of enclosing the Lincoln fields and commons was raised.

As you see from the map, most of the arable fields lay to the north of the city, and in the early nineteenth century they covered an area of about 1,734 acres. According to Domesday Book, Lincoln had about 1,851 acres of ploughed land, which is described as being " in the plain without the city." Under an Act passed in 1803 this land was divided up into enclosed fields, the common rights over it were extinguished, and the owners could sell their holdings for building purposes if they so wished. The Award under this Act was signed in 1811, and enrolled in 1815. Thus one of the obstacles to the growth of Lincoln was removed.

During the middle ages most of the meadow lands, or leys, of the city were on the slope of the hill to the west of the city, or on the hill side to the north of the Witham. The low lying land near the Fossdyke and upper Witham, and in the Witham gap, formed the common pasture lands.

The Carholme Common (135 acres) to the south of the Saxilby road, and the old West Common, or Ox Pasture (133 acres), to the north of the road, were used by householders living on the north side of the Witham. The Cowpaddle, then much more extensive than it is now, was used by all the citizens, and the South Common was shared by the villagers of Canwick and Lincoln citizens living to the south of High Bridge. The Swine Green was also common pasture land. These lands had been commons from a very early date.

THE STONEBOW
(As it appeared in 1836)

After the freemen had secured control of the city affairs, other commons were acquired and these were reserved for the use of the freemen. During the sixteenth century the swamps to the south of Brayford were gradually drained. At first islands (holmes) appeared. Cattle were taken to pasture by ferry boats. Later, when the swamps had been reduced to a few pools, the land became known as " the Holmes Common." After the dissolution of the monasteries, the city acquired the " Monks' Leys," which had been part of the property belonging to St. Mary's Abbey at York. A dispute between the new owners of the abbey lands and the city, concerning rights of common, led to the Monks' Leys being handed over to the freemen of the city. Under the Enclosure Act, 1803, a new West Common, containing the former Carholme, Ox Pasture and Short Leys, was laid out and made ready for use in 1805.

In the nineteenth century, part of the Monks' Leys Common was sold as building land, and in 1870 the rest was bought by the city corporation and converted into the Arboretum. The Holmes Common had already (c. 1853) been sold to the Great Northern Railway and parts of the South Common were sold to the same railway company in 1868 and 1891. The proceeds of these sales were used to provide a fund for the older freemen and their wives, who might be in need of assistance. When the freemen's grazing rights on the remaining commons were extinguished by the Lincoln Corporation Act in 1915, compensation for these rights was given and used to increase the freemen's funds, from which annuities of about £9 a year are paid. There are still about 250 names on the freemen's roll, but the number steadily declines.

TRANSPORT.

The enclosure of the open fields in 1811 is a sign of the times. It is one of many, for Lincoln was stirring with new life, but the one

The Arboretum was opened 26th August 1872 and extended in 1894 and again in 1953.

A Freemen's Guild was formed in 1970 to stimulate interest and new freemen have been enrolled.

that probably stood out most prominently to the people of the time was the great change that had taken place in the methods of transport. It dates back to the middle of the eighteenth century, when, in 1751, Squire Dashwood erected Dunston Pillar, a lighthouse, 70 feet high, to guide travellers over the barren waste of Lincoln Heath. It served as a landmark by day and a lighthouse by night. For more than thirty years the lantern at the summit was lighted regularly every night, but in the meantime other improvements had taken place and it was no longer so necessary.

Above all, the Turnpikes had begun. Five years after the erection of the Dunston Pillar, the road over Lincoln Heath was handed over to Turnpike Trusts. They undertook to keep it in repair from Dunsby Lane, near Cranwell, through the city, to Riseholme Hedge Corner, and Carholme Gate. Other roads near the city were also taken over at the same time, e.g., from Saxilby Bridge to Littleborough Ferry, from Brace-bridge to the City, and from Cranwell Hill over the South Common to the Great Bargate. An Act was passed to enable the Trustees to set up toll gates, and the tolls were fixed as follows :—

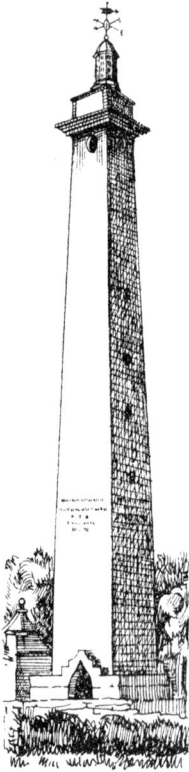

Dunston Pillar before the lantern was replaced by a statue of George III

For every horse, mule, ass, ox, or other beast of draught—1½d.
For every drove of oxen, cows or neat cattle—5d. per score.
For every drove of calves, hogs, sheep, lambs—2½d. per score.

Dunston Pillar was reduced in height in 1940 and the statue of George III removed. It is to be partly restored and placed in the grounds of Lincoln Castle.

Local farm traffic was excused payment altogether, though each farmer was expected to do three days' work on the road every year. Empty farm waggons returning from the Lincoln markets were also allowed free passage.

With the money thus collected, the Trustees were expected to keep the roads in good repair, a task which was made all the more difficult by the continuous increase in the traffic.   Gradually a regular service of coaches and carriers' carts was built up between Lincoln and all the neighbouring towns, and by 1810 there was a daily service of coaches to London.   In addition there were carriers' waggons conveying merchandise, two of which left for London every week.   They completed the journey in four days.   By 1833 the speed of travelling had greatly improved.   It was possible to reach Scarborough by coach in a day, and by using the railway for part of the journey, London could be reached in less than twelve hours.   The traveller picked up the " Royal Mail Coach " at the Saracen's Head at 6-30 in the evening, and travelled via Bourne and Deeping to Peterborough.   From here he took the train for London, arriving at Euston at six in the morning.   There was also a service by day via Kettering and Northampton, which took somewhat longer.   The Saracen's Head must have been a busy place a century ago.   The Royal Mail to London left at 6-30 in the evening, and another Royal Mail left for Hull at a quarter to eight in the morning, another to Grantham at one, and another to Nottingham at five. The " Tally Ho " coach left for London at 9 a.m., the " Imperial " to Nottingham and Newark at twelve noon, and to Hull at 2-15, the " Defiance " to Louth at 3 p.m., and the " Pelham " at five in the morning for Masborough via Rotherham.   All these had to be got off to the minute, since many of them were running in con-junction with the train services.   What a clatter of hoofs, what a tooting of horns, what a smell of sweating horses, as coach after

The Saracen's Head, south of the Stonebow, was sold for business premises in 1959.

coach roared in, and coach after coach pulled out, hour after hour, winter and summer alike. These were the great coaching days, the days of Tom Brown and Mr. Pickwick.

They were also the days of the steam packets on the Witham, of speed trials of paddle boats of rival firms. Towards the end of the eighteenth century great improvements had been made in the navigation of the Witham. The river was widened and deepened. New locks, weirs and sluices were constructed, and in order to accommodate the increased traffic between Boston and Lincoln, a service of horse-drawn boats was begun towards the end of the eighteenth century. By 1825 the horse had been replaced by the steam engine, and the firm of West and Clayton—Commodore West and Nathaniel Clayton, of whom we shall hear again—was running steam packets between the two towns. In 1829 a new type of paddle wheel invented by a Lincoln man, Mr. Poole, was fitted to the boats, and competition for the trade became intense. The journey was usually accomplished in the day. It might have been done still more quickly if the authorities responsible for maintaining the banks had not fixed a speed limit of four and a half miles an hour for part of the river below Lincoln. For the rest of the trip a speed of six miles an hour was attained. In 1836 a further advance was made when the first iron boat was launched at Boston, but in spite of these changes and improvements, the steam packet, like the coach, was doomed. In 1846 the railway came. In the same year a railway company obtained control of the waterway. It used its power to strike a severe blow at the river traffic. It deliberately allowed the channel to fall into neglect. It also put on fourth class carriages at a halfpenny a mile, and so drove the steam packets off the river.

Another ancient waterway came under the control of the railway at this time. This was the Fossdyke, of which an interesting story

FROM
Lincoln to Boston
AND BACK,
IN ONE DAY.

THE

FAVORITE,
CAPTAIN TEMPERTON,

A Poster advertising a Witham Steamer

may be told. Dug by the Romans, and used by the Danes, it had fallen into disrepair by the time of Henry I. It was repaired and restored to use in his reign, but as Lincoln declined in the later middle ages, so did the Fossdyke. In the reign of James I attempts were made to restore it, but very little seems to have been done. Nevertheless traffic increased, especially the carriage of coals and ale from Nottinghamshire via the Trent, and in 1741 the corporation, as we have seen, accepted the offer of Mr. Richard Ellison to lease it for 999 years, on condition that he should undertake to deepen the channel so that boats drawing three feet of water could pass from the Trent to Lincoln. The canal was afterwards neglected. The Fossdyke was of enormous importance to Lincoln at this time. It carried wheat and barley into the West Riding and Lancashire, flour to Manchester, wool to Huddersfield, Halifax and Leeds, and cattle to Manchester and Rotherham. In return the city received coal, lime, cotton, linen and woollen goods. In 1827 an appeal was made to Colonel Ellison to improve the canal. He refused. Neither would he lower the tolls. As was the case with the Witham navigation, however, the railway cast envious eyes upon it, and in 1846 the Ellison family sold the lease to the Great Northern Railway Company. The Fossdyke is still one of the most important trade arteries of the city.

The Coming of the Railways.

During these years England was being slowly, but surely, covered by a network of railways. Originally they were railways and nothing more, that is, a special kind of track upon which anyone could put a vehicle by paying a toll, just as anyone could put a boat on the canal or river, or a coach on a turnpike road. But the inconveniences of such a system were so serious that Railway Companies gradually took over the conveyance of goods and passengers as well as the provision of the permanent way. But there was dreadful confusion still. There were hundreds and thousands of separate companies promoting hundreds and thousands of little railways, and the poor passengers had to thread their way as best they could through a maze of different systems that would reduce a modern traveller to despair. But gradually the big towns were linked up. The big companies swallowed up the little ones, and through terrible slumps and booms, through mad speculation and financial crash, a workable system was at length evolved.   This was very largely the work of one remarkable man, George Hudson, an unscrupulous speculator with other people's money, but at the same time a man with the vision to see the outlines of a national system of railways.   He was largely responsible for the decision of the Midland Railway Company to build a line from Nottingham to Lincoln.   Lincoln was one of the last of the big towns to be brought into the railway network, and when the railway boom of 1843 began there was great competition among the different companies to be the first in the field.   There was not a single line of railway between the Ouse and the Humber at this time.   It was an agricultural district with no very large towns, and speculators had preferred to invest their money in the more densely populated parts of the country, but these were now fairly well served.   Lincolnshire was the most valuable prize still remaining to be divided up.   Who was to get in first ?   Was it to be the Company which was projecting a line from Wakefield to Boston, or the London—York line, or a Midland line?   Great issues were at stake among the local speculators and tremendous feeling was aroused.   A meeting of 6,000 people in the Cattle Market ended up in a free fight, when the mayor, who was chairman, declared in favour of the London to York project.   Its opponents said that the majority had consisted of labourers, hired at 2/- apiece, to hold up their hands in favour of the line.   On the other hand, George Hudson, the " Railway King," is known to have spent considerable sums of money in opposing it.   He had boasted that he would bring a railway to Lincolnshire before others had done talking about it, and apparently he was successful.   At any rate, the London to York line took a route west of Lincoln and the Midland Railway from Nottingham, in which Hudson was specially interested, was the first to reach the city.

It was opened in 1846 amid great rejoicing. The first train to run on the line pulled out of Nottingham at 9 a.m., and as it called at the village stations to pick up the lucky persons invited to take part, the church bells rang, flags fluttered from the steeples, the village bands struck up a merry tune, the labourers straightened their backs in the fields and the cattle scampered in fright. It reached Lincoln at 11 o'clock.

The Great Northern Railway from Peterborough to Lincoln followed in 1848, and so Lincoln High Street was crossed twice. Could not the two railways have combined to use the same crossing ? So Lincoln thought, and the Town Clerk was sent to London to try to persuade them to do so, but he was solemnly assured that not the slightest inconvenience need be anticipated. There would be no accidents and no serious detention of traffic ; and he came home convinced. It was not long, however, before Lincoln had cause to think otherwise.

THE GROWTH OF MODERN INDUSTRY.

Lincoln could now be reached by road, river, canal and railway. Trade poured into the city from all sides, and out again to all parts of England, and to many parts of the outside world, too. The stage was set for the latest phase of the city's growth, and for the establishment of entirely new industries by which a large part of the city lives today. Let us see how this last chapter of Lincoln's history came to be written.

It starts with the rise of Clayton and Shuttleworth's works. We have already met Nathaniel Clayton. He was one of the chief owners of the steam packets that plied for hire between Boston and Lincoln. He kept his boats in a channel of the river which used to connect the river with Sincil Dyke, near Stamp End Lock. Here was Joseph Shuttleworth's little shipbuilding yard. On one occasion, about 1842, Shuttleworth was a passenger on Clayton's boat, and owing to a breakdown, the two men had to spend the night in an inn at Tattershall. That night they came to an agreement which altered the course of Lincoln's history. By the decision which they then took, Lincoln was changed from a busy agricultural market town, into an industrial centre employing thousands of workmen, from which goods were sent to all parts of the world.

They agreed to go into partnership as iron founders. They could no doubt see that the coming of the railway would mean the ruin of the river traffic in which both men were so closely interested. At the same time, the railway brought new opportunities as well as dangers. Above all, it made possible the development of the engineering industry. Iron ore was found locally, and iron bars and sheets could be brought by rail. There was a growing market among the farmers, both at home and abroad, who were using more and more machinery, and the railways made possible for the first time the rapid transport of heavy goods to all parts of the country, and of workers to man the machines. We can imagine the drift of their conversation by the fireside of the Tattershall inn on that fateful night in 1842.

They bought a piece of land on the west side of the boat yard, and built on it a small works for boat repairing and the manufacture of iron pipes. But this was only a beginning. By 1847 they were employing about a hundred people, and they then turned their attention to the manufacture of portable steam engines and threshing machines—an epoch-making decision, by which they might win a brilliant success or lose all. The problem was how to find the necessary capital. A local firm of corn merchants and millers, Keyworth and Seely, gallantly came to their rescue with a bank guarantee in exchange for shares in the business, and three years later they produced their first agricultural steam engine. By 1854, when the Royal Agricultural Society visited Lincoln, the firm employed 600 men and it was described as the largest manufactory of steam engines in the world! Other firms followed in rapid succession. John Cooke, a farmer's son, apprenticed to a village wheelwright, founded the Lindum Plough works in 1851. Robey and Co's. works were founded in 1854, Newsum's and Foster's in 1856, and finally, in 1857, Joseph Ruston, Burton and Proctor established their foundry. All kinds of engines and machines were produced, and in 1860 we read of one of Robey's traction engines being tested on Canwick Hill. It not only went up, it also came down again with complete satisfaction, but it required a horse in the shafts to steer it!

But the most important development was the making of threshing machines. How many of us could write the history of the threshing machine? Yet it is one of the finest achievements of man's ingenuity. For thousands of years men were content to use flails to beat the corn from the ears and to leave it to the evening wind to blow away the chaff, or they drove an ox round and round the threshing floor to tread out the grain. Then in that great period of scientific invention, the seventeenth century, we first hear of experiments with flails worked by a crank. In the middle of the eighteenth century a Scotsman thought of shaking out the grain by putting the corn into a revolving drum. Finally in 1786 beaters were added to the revolving drum and the modern threshing machine in its simplest form came into being. It was carried about from place to place on a waggon and worked by hand or by a horse, but in 1841 an Ipswich firm began to manufacture self-moving steam threshing machines, and it was these that the enterprising firm of Clayton and Shuttleworth began to produce in 1847.

Many other firms, as we have seen, took part in the industrial revival of Lincoln at this time, and their history would be well worth telling, if only we had space to print it. The story of one firm, Foster's, can be told, at least in outline, and is as romantic as any in Lincoln's history. From grinding flour to the manufacture of tanks in the Great War ; that briefly is the history of Foster's. Like several other Lincoln firms, " Foster's " began as a flour mill, though no one knows exactly when. They were grinding flour long before 1856, when they first started to build threshers. They had already brought the first Watt's beam engine to the city in order to drive their mill—a tribute to their enterprise. In 1856 they set up a small foundry and began to build threshers and portable steam engines. They soon gave up flour milling and by 1865 they had converted their whole premises into an engineering works. They went on to establish a branch at Budapesth to make agricultural machinery for the farmers of central Europe, and then to build ships and torpedo boats to sail on the Danube. In 1889 the Lincoln works was turned into a Limited Liability Company as more capital was needed, and in 1900 the business was transferred from Waterside to Boultham and the old works sold to Rainforths.

From 1914 to 1918 they helped to equip the British army in the Great War, and in particular they earned fame by producing the first tanks.

There have been many changes in industry in Lincoln since 1945. Fosters became Allen Gwynnes and later moved from Lincoln. Ruston and Hornsby is now English Electric Diesels, Ltd. Newsums timber works is now A.E.I. Semiconductors, Ltd.

CHAPTER XXII.

SOCIAL SERVICES.

THE COMING OF MODERN LINCOLN.

From windmill to the tank in less than a century. This sums up the history of engineering in Lincoln. It is also a measure of the progress of the city. From a quiet country town of less than 8,000 inhabitants in 1800, it had grown in 1900 to be an important industrial centre of nearly 50,000. Between 1841 and 1881 the population increased by 24,000. This was the period of the coming of the railways and the beginning of large scale engineering.

So rapid a rise of population would obviously create many serious problems, housing, sanitation and water supply, for instance. The first question we must ask is—where did the new population live ? Indeed, it was a question which they often asked themselves. " The Lincolnshire Chronicle " of 1856 says, " Population is increasing so rapidly that houses, large, medium or small, are not to be had, and as a consequence, the more avaricious of the house-owners are raising rents." There was also a shortage of building land, and the price of building sites was high. The result was that houses were packed together as closely as possible. Is this the cause of the slum problem of which we have heard so much of late ? Not altogether. For this we must go further back, to the time when Lincoln was still a quiet country town with country sights and sounds, with orchards and gardens in the heart of the city, and plenty of land all round, one would have thought, to give ample room for everybody.

The strange thing is, the slums of Lincoln began *before* the growth of the big industries we spoke of above, when the population was still less than 10,000. But it was growing, as we have seen, owing to the progress of agriculture and the development of transport by land and water. More and more people were wanting houses, so Mr. Brown, or Mr. Jones, remembered the garden by the side of his house, and proceeded to run up a row of houses from end to end, or better still, two rows facing one another, or even back to back. No matter, so long as the greatest number of houses was put on the smallest possible space. Of course, there were no underground sewers, only a simple drain or an open channel down the middle leading into the road, or possible into the Witham ! That is the history of Jones' Row or Brown's Court.

But, you may ask, did the city council allow this kind of thing ? Of course they did. It never occurred to them to do otherwise. We should remember they had a very different idea of their duties from what a modern town council has. Until 1835, when the Municipal Corporations Act was passed and town government was made democratic, the city council was mainly concerned with looking after its property, and controlling the markets and the commons. The members were not the representatives of the community. They were the trustees of the freemen, who were alone entitled to the name of citizens. Even after 1835, when all rate-paying householders had the vote, it was long before they felt any collective responsibility for such questions as sanitation and water supply. These were matters for individuals to settle for themselves, but unless something was done there was real danger of disease, especially the dreaded cholera, and eventually the new corporation appointed a Sanitary Committee, and also an engineer to give expert advice. In 1849 he told them that the district known as the Drapery was very liable to disease, owing to the fact that houses, piggeries, privies and cesspools were packed together without proper drainage or ventilation, but nothing was done. The Public Health Act of 1848 had given the town councils powers to act in cases of this kind, but Lincoln decided not to use them. In 1859 a meeting was held in the Corn Exchange to discuss the question of introducing a proper drainage system, but the meeting decided to postpone the matter. An amendment was moved protesting against the crowded state of the houses, which prevented ventilation, poisoned the atmosphere, obscured the sun and caused sickness and death to spread among the poor who had the misfortune to live in them, but the mover of the amendment was shouted down by his fellow citizens, who no doubt lived in more salubrious parts of the town.

And so the slums went on. In fact they got worse, since the older they became the less fit they were to live in. Other improvements were gradually, but all too slowly, adopted. The new streets and courts were gradually paved. By 1875 a drainage scheme was being carried out, but the question of water supply continued to be postponed until 1908.

How had Lincoln been supplied before ? First, by means of the old Roman conduit, and later by the conduits laid by the friars and taken over by the corporation at the time of the Reformation. Then there were several public wells, one at the junction of Langworth Gate and Greetwell Gate, another at the north-east corner of the cathedral, and another in The Chequer Square. There were also several public pumps. Great things were hoped from the reservoir that was built at Hartsholme in 1848, but the water was said to be " stinking and impure . . . and only fit for washing floors and horses' feet with." It was polluted with sewage matter and was obviously unfit for use, but the new houses had no other supply so they continued to use it for another forty years. Then in 1886,

Dr. Harrison, the City Medical Officer, reported that the infant mortality was three times the average for the country, and he also pointed out that insufficient scavenging and the pollution of the water by sewage were liable to lead to epidemic diseases. A reader of the " Lincolnshire Chronicle " asked the corporation if anything was being done. Four years later a committee was appointed which reported that the water was only " fair second class " in quality, but the town had to go on drinking it for another twenty years. The climax came in 1905 with a severe attack of typhoid, and in 1908 the Elkesley Water Works were begun, in spite of the opposition of the diehards, and on October 4th, 1911, the new supply of fresh, pure water, which everybody could use, was turned on. Lincoln had at last caught up with the Romans !

FIRE FIGHTING SERVICES.

About the same time the city acquired an efficient fire engine. The control of fire had long been a matter of concern to the city authorities. In Elizabeth's reign they ordered the parishes to provide water buckets for carrying water and clamps of iron for tearing thatch from the roofs, but in the eighteenth century householders who could afford it insured against fire with the insurance companies, and the companies fixed plates on premises for which they were responsible. These plates may still be seen on No. 25 Steep Hill, 83 Bailgate, and elsewhere. At first, each company took care to put out only the fires on property for which it was responsible, and to leave other fires to be dealt with by the public, or not at all, but in time they began to see the advantages of co-operation. The Municipal Corporations Act of 1835 placed the responsibility of fire fighting once more upon the city. A watch committee was appointed which bought a fire engine, consisting of a pump worked by hand—a " manual " fire engine—and the duty

Lincoln now falls into the area of the Lincoln and District Water Board.

of putting out fires was handed over to the constables. In 1902 a number of them were specially trained and formed into a Fire Brigade. In 1882 a steam fire engine was bought, but it was drawn by horses, and it was not until 1910 that a modern locomotive fire engine was installed. This was felt to be desirable after a disastrous fire in the Minster Yard, which continued to burn because the horses which were used to draw the fire engine could not be found !

GAS AND ELECTRICITY.

The age-old methods of lighting by candles and lamps began to give place to gas in 1828, when the Gaslight and Coke Company was formed. It was taken over by the corporation in 1885, and completely re-equipped in 1933. By that time it had the rivalry of electricity to meet. In 1898 a generating station was erected at Brayford side, but the larger industrial works had been making their own electricity for power lighting for some years before this time. During the Great War (1914–1918) the development in the use of electricity went on very rapidly, and when it was over, the city authorities bought the plant of Messrs. Clayton and Shuttle-worth, and made large extensions which brought electricity into almost every street in the city, and ensured a supply to any citizen who wanted it.

PUBLIC TRANSPORT.

With the growth of population and the establishment of new industries employing thousands of workers, the problem of transport became acute. A tramway round Brayford was suggested as early as 1855, but it was not until 1882 that the Lincoln Tramway Company laid a track from Bracebridge to St. Benedict's Square. The trams were drawn by horses, and the journey took twenty minutes.

A modern fire station with all the latest equipment was built on South Park Link Road in 1964.

Gas and electricity are now supplied by nationalised Boards.

The South West Profpect of Lincoln Caftle.

To Tomcent Amcotts Efq.r High Sheriff
of the County of Lincoln this prefent Year 1727, and
Governor of this Caftle
This Profpect is most gratefully Infcribed by
His Obedient Hum.: Serv.t
Sam.l Buck —

THERE was undoubtedly a Caftle with many Forts Built here
by the Romans and repaired by the Saxons, &c in the
reading; Cies as it, Sart in need from the Sundry; Sieges
it fuftained; Repair'd particularly by King William I.st
after that Conquest over King Harold.

THE CASTLE
(As it appeared in 1726)

A Lincoln Tram in 1904

The corporation bought the undertaking in 1904 and electrified it a year later, but within a quarter of a century this service of electric trams was entirely superseded. In 1929 the motor bus took its place, and the jangle of the tram—the most nerve shattering noise, perhaps, ever heard in the long history of Lincoln streets—was heard no more.

THE CORPORATION TODAY AND YESTERDAY.

All these changes bring out one startling fact; that the City Council is everywhere and in everything. It supplies water, light and heat. It carries us about our business and watches over our health. It builds many of our houses and educates most of our children, and every year that passes it adds to its burden. Until

The City no longer supplies water, light and heat.

1835 it could not even raise a rate. The individual parishes alone had this power, and the only rate they could levy was the Poor Rate. But even after 1835 the powers of the corporation were very limited. Nearly all public services—roads, water, gas, for instance—were looked after by independent boards and companies, and the work of poor relief was in the hands of an entirely separate body, the Guardians of the Poor. Gradually they were all absorbed by the corporation, especially after the Public Health Act of 1875. Instead of having separate authorities, each supplying a particular service and collecting its own revenue, they were brought under one great authority which, through its different departments, supplied the various services, and by means of its financial department, collected the revenue. In 1907 the nineteen civil parishes were amalgamated into the one civil parish of Lincoln, and in 1930 the last of the independent bodies, the Poor Law Guardians, was brought in. What a Colossus it is, this City Council ! And how vitally necessary it is that we should see that it does its multifarious duties properly.

TWO GREAT ENTERPRISES.

We have only to consider the work done by the city corporation in regard to housing and public health, and, perhaps especially, education, to realise the enormous part it plays in our lives. We have already seen the dreadful condition of the slums of Lincoln, and the apathy with which the problem was regarded for years and years by the older generation of city councillors, but by 1914 a desire for change and improvement had made itself felt. An Act had been passed in 1890 to enable the local councils to take this action, but it was not until the eve of the Great War (1914–1918) that Lincoln decided to put it into force. Then the Great War came and held up all progress. In 1919 another Act of Parliament was passed—the Housing and Town Planning Act—and this time the council acted more promptly. By March 1935, 1,544 houses had been built at a total cost of £875,552. That does not mean that all housing problems are at an end in Lincoln. Indeed, new problems are arising as fast as the old ones are solved. For instance—what is the effect of moving people from the centre of the town to a new housing estate at a greater distance from their employment ? Does the advantage of a better house outweigh the extra cost of transport ? Do the new housing estates require organised centres in order to develop their community life, and if so, is it to be done through the schools or in some other way ?

Closely connected with the progress in housing is the question of public health. Here the change is nothing short of revolutionary. In 1866 a part-time Medical Officer of Health was appointed and his salary was £15 a year ! We may be sure he earned it, especially when we realise that it was largely due to his pressure that the council was persuaded to set up a fever hospital in 1903-4. In 1910 a health visitor was appointed and from these two modest beginnings has sprung the amazing growth of public health services operating today—infant welfare centres, dental clinics, dispensaries, maternity centres, and Medical Services—all under the control of the city's Medical Officer of Health.

INDUSTRY AFTER THE GREAT WAR (1914–1918).

But behind the story of the wonderful growth of our local social services lurks a great shadow. That is the problem of unemployment.

It was not unknown in Lincoln before the Great War. We have heard of it already as far back as Elizabeth's reign ; and during all the subsequent periods there were a few people who had to rely on the poor rates for existence. It was very serious in the early years of the twentieth century.

The post-war housing programme has greatly extended the Corporation Estates which now include houses mainly built in the north at Ermine and in the south-west at Hartsholme, Boultham Moor and Birchwood. Approximately 9200 houses built by Lincoln Corporation.

Some health services, including maternity, are now under the National Health Service.

After the Great War, Lincoln firms found themselves in difficulties. Orders for war materials had stopped and old markets had been lost.   Russia and the Argentine had ceased to buy threshing machines and engines from England.

Let us take a well-known Lincoln case.   Round about the year 1842, the famous firm of Clayton and Shuttleworth began its wonderful and tragic career.   From its humble forge in Stamp End it began to send out its products all over the world—to Odessa, Riga, Budapesth, Paris, to Egypt, Argentine, Java and Chile.   In these and many other places it had its agencies.   What firm was more securely based ?   It seemed as safe as the Bank of England.   The overseers and supervisors, the aristocracy of Lincoln workmen, did their rounds from shop to shop on horseback.   They were " collar and tie gents," and were expected to sport a tall hat, and the founder of the firm, Nathaniel Clayton, was " Natty " to all his men ; a family firm, if ever there was one.   In 1901 it became a limited company. Soon there were difficulties in foreign countries where war was in the air and the price of shares fell.   In 1914 war came.   During the war trade boomed, but afterwards there came a slump, and in 1931 complete collapse.   A notice was put up " For Sale."   The workmen were thrown out of work and many of them had to face years of unemployment.   Fortunately for Lincoln the engineering firms lost no time in seeking for new markets and producing articles which they had not made before, but for which there was still a demand.   Ruston's increased their production of excavators ; Foster's turned to the manufacture of pumps ; and by adopting new methods and producing a wider variety of machines they re-established themselves in the world markets.

In September, 1922, there were 6,600 unemployed persons in Lincoln.   By September, 1927, this figure had been reduced to

1,000, which was regarded as the normal for the city. Then came a great trade depression and in March, 1933, no fewer than 7,700 persons were unemployed. The worst effects of this slump gradually passed away, and the time must surely come when this problem will vanish altogether.

CHAPTER XXIII.

WAR RETURNS TO LINCOLN

In 1938 the international situation became so uncertain that it was necessary to prepare for the possibility of another war with Germany. If this came, Lincoln might be attacked from the air, and no one could be sure that gases would not be used against the city. Civil Defence services were prepared and volunteers were enrolled to act as special constables, wardens and ambulance drivers, and to work in first aid parties and in rest and information centres after raids.

The situation was so serious that gas masks were issued and trenches were dug on the West and South Commons and in the Monks Abbey grounds for use as shelters during air raids.

After the Munich agreement it was hoped for a time that war had been avoided, but in 1939 the struggle with Germany began. This again brought death by acts of war to the streets of the city after three hundred years of freedom from armed violence. During the first World War (1914–1918) Zeppelins had dropped bombs at Greetwell, but the city itself had been untouched by active warfare since the Civil Wars in the seventeenth century.

On the outbreak of war, children from Leeds were brought to Lincoln, which was believed to be a safer area. Arrangements for dealing with the consequences of air attacks were made, and constantly revised and improved throughout the war. Gas masks were provided for all and kept in repair. Morrison and Anderson shelters were issued, basements were strengthened for use as public shelters, and brick shelters were built for householders on waste land, in gardens, and even on the highways. The citizens were warned of the approach of enemy aircraft by sirens, and, during the war, they spent many anxious hours listening to German planes flying over the city to raid Sheffield and Liverpool.

Perhaps the most troublesome of all the precautions made necessary by the war was the " black-out." A carelessly-drawn curtain would, within a few minutes, attract a visit from the police or air raid wardens, and only the flashes from hand torches or the dimmed lights of passing motor cars and cycles relieved the blackness of the streets. In the absence of enemy aircraft in the vicinity a single red light floated from the highest tower of the cathedral—a warning signal to our own aeroplanes, but an emblem of temporary security to the anxious citizens groping in the darkness below.

When the full extent of the danger from fire was realised, the able-bodied men and women of the city were organised into parties of fireguards to keep constant watch in the streets and on business premises.

As in the previous war, the engineering works of Lincoln were soon fully engaged in producing munitions and supplies for the armed forces. Unemployment rapidly disappeared from the city.

The first fatal casualty in the city occurred on 24th March, 1941, when a stick of bombs, dropped by a lone raider at 3-45 a.m., destroyed St. Swithin's School and houses in Coningsby Street and Baggholme Road.

Another single plane destroyed Cold Bath House and damaged the Nurses' Home at the County Hospital, when most of the citizens were sitting down to their teas on the Sunday evening before the August Bank Holiday in 1942.

The heaviest attack on the city took place on 15th January, 1943. It was heralded by a huge semicircle of flares placed round the northern side of the city and six high-explosive bombs, three phosphorous bombs, and eight fire-pots were dropped on the city causing fires, damage to houses, and casualties in a bus. A bomb which dropped in Thomas Street, and did not explode until several hours later, destroyed several houses after the inhabitants had left them. Thirty persons were injured and four killed.

Incendiary bombs were dropped on the city on several occasions and " butterfly " bombs, larger anti-personnel bombs, and machine-gun fire from planes were all used against it. A flying bomb (V1) passed over Lincoln at 5-30 a.m. on Christmas Eve, 1944.

The sirens warned the city of approaching danger 238 times, and bombs were dropped by the enemy on 18 occasions, causing 11 deaths and wounding 54 people. Thirty-nine houses were destroyed and 2,343 were damaged.

There were many aerodromes near the city and accidents to aeroplanes flying over or near the houses added another risk to life in Lincoln. During the war six planes crashed inside the city boundaries, killing 9 and injuring 22 civilians, in addition to causing the deaths of 18 members of their crews.

St. Matthias' Church was damaged by a falling plane on 8th September, 1940, and the High School Boarding House on Greestone Stairs was wrecked on 22nd July, 1941. On Sunday, 27th July, 1941, two planes collided in mid-air. One fell in Drake Street and the other struck a row of houses in Oxford Street, killing three people and injuring nine. A bomber which crashed in Highfield Avenue in June, 1943, caused five fatal casualties to civilians.

In spite of all this damage, when the citizens of Lincoln remember the havoc caused elsewhere, they may well be thankful that during the war their own city lost none of its ancient treasures, and that their glorious cathedral still stands undamaged on the hill where it has stood and, we hope, will continue to stand, through many centuries.

HISTORICAL BUILDINGS OF LINCOLN.

THE CASTLE.

In 1068 William the Conqueror took steps to secure his possession of England by building castles in several important towns, including Lincoln, York and Nottingham.

We must not imagine that the castle was immediately planned to be built as we know it. Like the cathedral, it grew and developed piece by piece, and each addition shows improvements in style suggested by experience gained in actual warfare. The style of the defences altered as the means of attacking them increased in power and effectiveness, and each advance in the design of offensive weapons brought improvements in the art of building castles. At Lincoln the Normans found a strong defensive position on the top of the hill, with a large space, the upper Roman city, already walled and moated, and easy to hold. William put the whole of this enclosure under the control of the officer holding the castle, who was known as the constable, and this area formed the outer " Bailey " or " Bail " of the castle.

The south-western quarter of the Roman enclosure was cleared and strengthened by the construction of the castle itself. Like other strongholds of that period this consisted of a space enclosed by great earthworks, with one or more high mounds, on which stood towers. A wall ran along the crest of the earthworks, and this, like the towers, may have been of wood. The earthworks at Lincoln completely buried the Roman west gate and part of the western Roman wall. The castle has now two mounds, but we do not know that they were both thrown up when the castle was first constructed. It is probable that the south-eastern mound, on which the observatory tower stands, is the earlier, and was placed where it would overlook the city because the castle was intended to control the town, not to defend it from outside attack.

As the castle stood on a dry limestone rock, it was impossible to surround it with water, but when the earthworks were thrown up wide and deep ditches were formed outside the castle.

In order to secure a garrison certain lands were held by the tenants on condition that they should supply knights to guard the castle for a definite number of days in the year. In time it became the custom to pay a " castle guard rent " instead of sending men.

As the earthworks and mounds settled and became firm, it was possible to replace stockades and wooden buildings by a stone curtain wall and tower. This had been done at Lincoln by 1115. A rectangular stone keep was built on the mound near the eastern castle gateway. The lower walls of this tower are still standing. The curtain wall contains good examples of Norman " herring bone work."

Two gate houses were also built, one in the western wall leading into the open country, and one in the eastern wall, leading into the city. The western gateway, sometimes called " the sallyport," now gives us a good idea of the original appearance of these entrances to the castle. They were built with rectangular corners and great round arches for the gates.

Experience soon taught castle builders that square towers and sharp corners in a castle were easily destroyed. It was not difficult to force stones out of the corners when the joints of the masonry were parallel, and, this being so, the corners were the points which invited attack. At the same time the angle of a tower was the most difficult spot to defend by shooting arrows through the loopholes in the wall. Accordingly a new type of keep was invented. It was a many-sided enclosure on the top of a mound. The angles in the wall were very blunt. It had no roof but there were timber buildings close to the wall leaving the centre open to the sky. Such a building is known as a " shell keep," and one was erected on a second mound at Lincoln castle, which had been originally fortified by the Countess Lucy, a great landholder in Lincolnshire. The king must have given permission for the second keep to be built, and Countess Lucy and her descendants were allowed to hold it for him. The shell keep came to be known as " The Lucy Tower." In later years this name was also used for the tower on Brayford.

The Crusades led to a great improvement in the art of fortification in Western Europe. Castle builders learned to round off all sharp corners and make their towers circular. The keep had been the chief feature of the early castles, but experience led military architects to pay much more attention to the curtain wall, which they learned to defend by round flanking towers rising above the rampart walk. The defences of the gates were also increased.

At Lincoln castle great improvements were possible. The old Norman gatehouses had never been very strong. A new front, having a pointed arch and two turrets, was added to the eastern gate, and both entrances were strengthened by the building of new barbicans. At the Castle Hill gateway strong walls were built out on each side of the gate forming a narrow passage, the entrance to which was closed by an outer gate between two round towers, which stood within the moat. The barbican of the western entrance appears to have been less elaborate.

To a knight of the thirteenth century, who had fought in Palestine, the Norman curtain wall at Lincoln would appear to be very weak, and obviously in need of flanking towers at its corners. A beginning was made towards supplying this want by the erection of Cob

Hall, which, in accordance with the practice of the time, presented a circular front to attackers. This tower was used in the middle ages as a prison. A prisoner, named Thomas Goddard, passed the weary hours in scratching a picture of a stag hunt on the wall of his cell. In the fourteenth century the old Norman keep on the south-east mound was also improved by the addition of a new front upon its east face. A range of narrow rooms or galleries was built against the wall of the castle between this tower and the eastern gate. These chambers, which have been demolished, occupied the usual position of the domestic buildings of a castle.

No further improvements were made to the fortifications of the castle, as no necessity for continuing the work ever arose at Lincoln.

The additions to the buildings of the castle at later dates were in connection with its use as a prison or for the administration of justice. During the middle ages a large building known as the " Shire House " was erected in the centre of the great courtyard. This was afterwards used for the Assizes and Quarter Sessions.

After the castle was taken by the Parliamentarians in 1644, it was made incapable of defence. Its battlements were thrown down and breaches were made in the walls, but it still served as a prison.

In 1787 a new prison was erected, which was partly rebuilt in 1846. These buildings ceased to be used as the County Gaol in 1878.

The entrance to the castle through the old barbican became inconvenient and unsafe, and in 1791 the approach was improved by taking down the barbican towers and two houses which partly blocked up the roadway to the castle.

At the beginning of the nineteenth century John Merryweather was Governor of the prison and interested in astronomy. He was responsible for the addition of the circular flag turret to the tower near the eastern gate. He kept his instruments here, and it became known as " the Observatory Tower."

During the eighteenth century Cob Hall had a conical thatched roof but this was replaced by a flat lead roof in 1815, when this tower was fitted up as a place of execution.

The present Assize Courts were built in 1826.

At first the castle was held for the king by the constables, whose rights in the castle later passed to the Earls of Lincoln and then to the Dukes of Lancaster. The castle was sold to the magistrates of the county in 1831.

THE CATHEDRAL.

From the seventh century to the tenth century there was a bishop of Lindsey. The site of his cathedral is not known with certainty but it may have been at Lincoln. The dioceses of Lindsey and Leicester were united with that of Dorchester in Oxfordshire. As we have seen, William the Conqueror made Remigius bishop of Dorchester, and gave him permission to move his seat to Lincoln and build a cathedral here (c. 1073).

In Chapter V we read how Bishop Hugh began to rebuild the Norman cathedral in a new style, now known as " Early English."

Bishop Grosseteste continued his work. He built the new screen surrounding the original Norman front, and also rebuilt the lower stage of the recently built central tower after it had fallen down in 1237. We have already heard how the Angel Choir was added, in a still richer style, to contain the shrine of St. Hugh.

By 1311 the cloisters and the upper stages of the Central Tower had also been added to the cathedral. They, like the Angel Choir, are built in the " Decorated " style.

Another change in architectural fashion began about the year 1360. Arches were flattened and perpendicular and horizontal lines took the place of flowing curves in the tracery of windows. This became known as the " Perpendicular " style, and the upper stages of the western towers were built in this way about the year 1390. The cathedral was then very much as we know it now, though small improvements and additions were made from time to time. In the fifteenth century, small Chantry Chapels were added. Bishop Fleming's dates from about 1430, and Bishop Russell's from about 1490. Windows in the perpendicular style were inserted in the Norman masonry of the west front, and new screens and monuments were added to beautify the interior. On each of the towers a tall spire of timber and lead was erected, and the interior was adorned by a number of shrines decorated with gold, silver and precious stones. By 1530 the cathedral was at the height of its glory.

But the wealth of the church had aroused the greed of the king. Henry VIII, after his break with Rome, stripped the church of its treasures. Shortly afterwards, in 1547, the spire on the central tower was blown down, and in 1548 the protestant zeal of Bishop Holbeach and George Heneage, the Dean, led to the removal and destruction of all the images of Christ, the Virgin and the Saints. In 1644, the soldiers of Parliament tore off the brasses from the tomb-stones, and destroyed much of the stained glass in the windows. The most important examples of medieval glass which survived are in the great rose windows of the western transept, known as " The Dean's Eye " and " The Bishop's Eye," the four windows under " The Bishop's Eye," and two windows at the east end of the cathedral.

After the Restoration the north side of the cloisters, which had become ruinous, was replaced by an arcade in the classical style, with a new library built over it. This improvement was designed by Sir Christopher Wren.

The spires on the western towers became unsafe. A riot was caused by a proposal to remove them in 1726, and they were saved for a time, but they were taken down in 1807. Another new library was the last important addition to the cathedral.

During the twentieth century the building has been thoroughly restored and is now perhaps the finest cathedral in England, in which every style of Norman and English Gothic architecture is blended into one harmonious whole.

ANCIENT GATEHOUSES.

The remains of walls and gatehouses to be found in Lincoln belong, as we have read, to three different defensive systems, the Roman city, the Close wall, and the medieval replacements of Roman work and walls for the protection of the suburbs.

The Stonebow is on or near the site of the south gate of the lower Roman city. It is probable that the Roman gatehouse was similar to Newport Arch, but we know nothing of its history. We do know that the greater part, at any rate, of the present building dates from after 1500, and we know that an arch with a room over it stood on the same site at a much earlier date. The " Stanbogh " is mentioned in the reign of John. The first hall mentioned in the city records in connection with meetings of the leading citizens was the " Guild Hall," which stood near the house of the Grey Friars, and was handed over to them in 1237 at the request of the king himself, who promised to provide a new room for transacting town business. The hall provided appears to have been the room in the gatehouse which stood where the Stonebow now stands. This hall became a nuisance to traffic. The arch was low, inconvenient and unsafe, and it was decided to rebuild it " loftier and more convenient for citizens and for strangers flocking thither with victuals." But some of the citizens were unwilling to contribute to the cost of the new hall. The other citizens appealed to the king, and in 1390 he authorised the mayor and bailiffs to compel the obstinate citizens to pay. The money was then collected but the hall was not built.

Three years later complaint was made that the collectors had used the money for the Guildhall for their own purposes. An enquiry into the scandal was held, and a suitable hall was at last provided, which served until 1520, when an agreement was made with William Spencer, freemason, and his fellows, for building the Guildhall. The main gateway probably dates from the fifteenth century. The side arches have been much altered. The upper storey, dating from about 1520, formerly had tracery of the perpendicular style in the windows. The ancient lights were damaged in an eighteenth century election riot, and the present windows are modern. The Royal Arms on the south side date from the Stuart period, and may have been placed on the Bow when James I visited Lincoln.

The ancient " Mote Bell " was cast in 1371. The eastern wing of the Stonebow was formerly used as a prison and kitchen. In 1586 the council decided to use " the house next to the prison called the Kitchen " as a prison for apprentices and persons committing small offences. Until 1809 these buildings served as the city prison, and the Guildhall was used as a court of justice where Quarter Sessions and Assizes were held. The contents of the Guildhall are of great interest.   In addition to the city insignia there are several paintings of Kings and Queens of England.

The Exchequer Gate, which was the inner gatehouse at the main entrance to the Close, dates from the reign of Edward I, though it has been much restored.   It is a good example of a gateway in the decorated style.   The hooks for the hinges of the doors and slots for the bars to fasten them may still be seen in the archways.   It

Pottergate Arch (North Side)

has been suggested that the walled-up openings in the walls of the passages through the gatehouse were the places where relics, beads and rosaries were once sold.

Pottergate Arch protected the southern entrance to the Close. It spanned the only roadway leading into the Close which was protected by a single gatehouse. Probably the steep slope of the ground was believed to make a second unnecessary. The Turnpike Road Act of 1777 gave the Turnpike Trustees power to purchase and demolish this gateway if necessary, but fortunately they did not exercise their powers. A little later, in 1794, a subscription was raised for pulling down the arch. To this the corporation voted twenty guineas, but again the gatehouse was saved. In later years the Bromhead family held the chamber over the arch until the house on the west side was demolished and its site used to widen the road. The upper storey of the building has been largely rebuilt.

One more of the original entrances to the Close still survives. This is the small postern at the head of the Greestone Stairs, which were originally named " The Greesen." This is early English for " The Steps." It was through this unguarded door that the mob entered the Close in 1726 to protest against a proposal to take down the spires on the western towers of the cathedral. The Chancellor opened his beer cellar and the rioters were soothed with promises that their wishes should be respected. The crowd dispersed and the spires were saved for a time.

The gates of the Close were locked at night until well into the eighteenth century.

The present Priory Gate reminds us of two gatehouses which formerly protected the northern entrance to the Close. One stood

The Old Registry or North Gate of the Close which occupied the side of
Priory Gate

near Eastgate, between " The Rest " and the site of the former inn
known as " The Dolphins." The other was where the present
arch stands. Both were used during the seventeenth century as
dwelling houses, and the inner gatehouse became the place where
the registers of the bishops and archdeacons of Lincoln, and the
records of the dean and chapter were kept. It was taken down in
1815 and the present gateway was built in 1816.

LIST OF AUTHORITIES.

The reader who wishes to learn more about subjects connected with the history of Lincoln will find much fuller details in the following books and articles than it has been possible to give in this book.

L.N. & Q.=Lincolnshire Notes and Queries.
A.A.S.R.=Associated Architectural and Archaeological Societies' Reports.

BATTLES OF 1141 AND 1217.

History of the Art of War in the Middle Ages. Charles Oman, Vol. I.

Collected Papers of T. F. Tout. Vol. II.

Minority of Henry III. K. Norgate.

Campaign and Battle of Lincoln, 1217. F. W. Brooks and F. Oakley, A.A.S.R., Vol. 36, p. 295.

BEAUMONT FEE.

The Manor of Hungate. J. W. F. Hill, A.A.S.R., Vol. 38, p. 167.

The Corporation of Lincoln. J. W. F. Hill, A.A.S.R., Vol. 37, p. 177.

BISHOPS.

List of Bishops to 1547 with notes on each. A.A.S.R., Vol. II.

BISHOP'S PALACE.

English Episcopal Palaces. Edited by R. S. Rait.

Article by E. J. Willson. Proceedings of Arch. Institute. Lincoln, 1848.

Article by the Rev. E. Venables. L.N. & Q., Vol. I.

CASTLE.

Guide to Castle. Morton, 1906.
Articles by the Rev. C. H. Hartshorne and E. J. Willson. Proceedings of Archaeological Institute at Lincoln, 1848.
Article by G. T. Clark. A.A.S.R., Vol. XIII.
The Constable and the Guard. J. W. F. Hill, A.A.S.R., Vol. 40, p. 1.
Drawings of Barbican Towers. Gough's Camden, 1806.

CATHEDRAL.

Lincoln—The Cathedral and See. Bell's Cathedral Series.
Story of Lincoln Minster. The Rev. J. H. Srawley, D.D.
Victoria County History.

CHURCHES.

Pre-Reformation Churches and Union of Parishes, 1549. The Rev. E. Venables, A.A.S.R., Vol. XIX, p. 326.

CIVIL WAR.

Article by the Rev. E. H. R. Tatham in " Memorials of Old Lincolnshire."
Articles by J. G. Williams. L.N. & Q., Vol. VIII.
Pamphlets in the City Library.

CLOSE.

Survey of Houses in the Close (Map). The Rev. E. Venables, A.A.S.R., Vol. XIX, p. 43.
The Corporation of Lincoln. J. W. F. Hill, A.A.S.R., Vol. 37, p. 177.
A Ramble through the Parish of St. Mary Magdalene, Lincoln. The Rev. A. R. Maddison, A.A.S.R., Vol. XXI, p 10.

DANISH AND NORMAN LINCOLN.
J. W. F. Hill, A.A.S.R., Vol. 41, p. 7.

EDUCATION.
GRAMMAR SCHOOL. Article on Grey Friary. E. Mansel Sympson,
L.N. & Q., Vol. 7.
Articles in Lincs. Magazine. Vol. 1, Nos. 11 and 12.
CHRIST'S HOSPITAL SCHOOL. Documents in the City Library.
Article by W. H. Goy in Lincs. Magazine, Vol. 3, No. 1.
Article by R. F. Dalton on Witton Dalton in Lincs. Magazine,
Vol. 3, No. 3.

ENCLOSURE.
Copy of Enclosure Act (1803) in City Library.
The Award at the City Library.

GENERAL HISTORY.
Medieval Lincoln. J. W. F. Hill.
Lincoln. E. Mansel Sympson.
Historical Manuscripts Commission, 14th Report, Appendix,
Part VIII, Manuscripts of Lincoln, etc.
Walks through Lincoln. The Rev. E. Venables.
Lincoln Date Book.

GILDS.
Parish Gilds in Medieval England. H. F. Westlake.
English Gilds. Toulmin Smith. Early English Text Society.
Historical Manuscripts Commission. 14th Report, Appendix,
Part VIII, Manuscripts of Lincoln.

GOVERNMENT OF CITY.
The Corporation of Lincoln. J. W. F. Hill, A.A.S.R., Vol. 37,
p. 177.

HIGH BRIDGE AND BRIDGE CHAPEL.

Report on High Bridge. W. Watkins and Son, 1902.
Article by the Rev. E. Venables, A.A.S.R., Vol. XIX, p. 334.

INSIGNIA.

Articles by J. G. Williams in Lincs. Notes and Queries. Vols. 6 and 7.

JEWS.

Transaction of Jewish Historical Society. Book II.
History of the Jews in England. A. M. Hyamson.
Jews of Angevin England. J. Jacobs.
Jews of Medieval Lincoln. M. D. Davies, Arch. Journ., XXXVIII.
Articles in Lincs. Notes and Queries. Vols. 2, 16 and 17.

" JOHN OF GAUNT'S PALACE."

Article by E. M. Sympson. L.N. & Q., Vol. VIII.

LINCOLNSHIRE REBELLION.

State Papers Henry VIII, Vol. 1, Part II, Letter 48 and Paper 51.
The Pilgrimage of Grace, 1536–1537. M. H. Dodds and R. Dodds.

MAYORS.

Three Lists of Mayors. J. W. F. Hill, A.A.S.R., Vol. 39, p. 217.

NONCONFORMITY.

Early Nonconformity in Lincoln. J. W. F. Hill.

PARLIAMENTS IN LINCOLN.

Article by the Rev. C. H. Hartshorne in Proceedings of the Arch. Inst. Lincoln, 1848.

PARISH ADMINISTRATION.

St. Peter-in-Eastgate in the Eighteenth Century. The Rev.
Canon A. M. Cook.

The Church and Parish of St. Paul-in-the-Bail. The Rev. E. R.
Milton.

RELIGIOUS HOUSES.

PRIORY OF ST. KATHARINE. The Rev. R. E. G. Cole, A.A.S.R.,
Vol. 27, Pt. II, p. 264.

GREY FRIARY. Article by E. Mansel Sympson. L.N. & Q.,
Vol. VII, No. 59.

Article by A. R. Martin. Archaeological Journal, Vol.
XCII, Pt. I, p. 42.

HOSPITAL OF THE HOLY INNOCENTS. F. W. Brooks, A.A.S.R.,
Vol. 42, p. 157.

GENERAL. Victoria County History.

Monasteries near the Witham. The Rev. J. A. Penny.

ROMAN LINCOLN.

Article by I. A. Richmond. Archaeological Journal, Vol. CIII,
p. 26.

Inscribed Stones. A. Smith.

Lincolnshire in Roman Times. Article by the Rev. E. H. R.
Tatham in " Memorials of old Lincolnshire."

Roman Lincoln. F. T. Baker.

Roman Colonnade in Bailgate. The Rev. E. Venables, A.A.S.R.,
Vol. 21, p. 3.

ST. MARY'S CONDUIT.

Paper by E. J. Willson in Proceedings of Arch. Inst. at Lincoln,
1848.

Article by A. Welby. L.N. & Q., Vol. XX.

TRIAL OF TEMPLARS.

Article by The Rev. G. Oliver in " Papers on the County of Lincoln."

Article by R. de la Bere in Lincs. Mag., Vol. 3, Nos. 1 and 2.

INDEX.

PAGE

Aaron 77
Aaron's House............. 78
Agriculture 189
Air Raids................. 214
Aldermen 171
Angel Choir 51, 60
Arboretum 193
Arthur, King 27
Askewe, Anne 127

Bacon, Roger 53
Bail 41, 178, 218
Bailgate 34
Baptists 147
Bargate, Great 32, 33, 41, 68, 194
— , Little 33, 143
Barrows.................. 12
Basilica 20
Battle, 1141................ 39
— , 1217................ 41
— , 1644................ 143
— , 1648................ 143
Bayeux, Ralph 185
Beaumont Fee 185
Becke, Robert.............. 139
Belasset of Wallingford 84
Bishop Alexander........... 46
—   Alnwick 66
—   Bloet 118
—   Burghersh, Henry de 133
—   Chesney 118
—   Dalderby 130
—   Grosseteste   51-53, 222
—   Holbeach 131, 223
—   Hugh of Avalon 47-51, 130
—   Hugh of Wells....... 40
—   Longland, John...... 66
—   Neile 67

PAGE

Bishop Remigius 36, 44, 115
—   Sutton 181
—   Taylor 134
—   Watson 134
—   Williams............ 137
Bishop's Palace....... 64-66, 144
Black Death 86
Blecca 28
Blind Well 20
Bluecoat School 158
Boston.................. 87, 122
Boundary Stones 180
Bracebridge 121
Branston 121
Brayford 33
Burgmanmot 38, 86
Burghersh, Bartholomew 132
—   Chantry........ 132
Burton Lazars 118
Butterwick 36

Cantilupe Chantry 133
Canute................... 30
Canwick 33, 121
—   Hill Gallows 82, 117, 129
Cardyke................... 23
Carholme 192
Castle........ 35, 143, 165, 218
Cathedral..36, 44, 60, 78, 130,
143, 144, 222
Celtic settlement 11, 15
—   words 27
Chantries....89, 95, 132, 133, 153
Chapter House........54, 61, 125
Charles I................141, 170
Charter 170
Chaucer, Geoffrey 56
Christianity................ 28

PAGE

Churches, Ancient.......... 135
City School................ 159
Clasketgate 56
Clayton, Nathaniel...... 196, 200
Clayton and Shuttleworth..200, 212
Close 180
Cloth Trade 90
Coaches................... 195
Cob Hall................221, 222
Colonies, Roman........... 16
Commons............32, 175, 192
Conduit, St. Mary's 111
Cooke, John 202
Cooper, Thomas 151
Copin 81
Corporation 167, 209
Courts............ 167, 178, 181
Cowpaddle 192

Danes 29
Deanery 142
Defoe.................... 190
Despencer................ 62
Dickenson, Roger 128
Domesday Book...........33, 36
Dorchester........... 35, 44, 222
Dunston Pillar 194

Earthquakes 38
Education 153
Edward the Elder.......... 30
—   I 59, 85
—   II 181
—   III 63
—   IV 63
Edwin 28
Eleanor, Queen.......... 61, 106
Electricity supply.......... 208
Ellison, Richard 176, 198
—   Colonel 177, 198
Enclosure Act............. 192
Ermine Street.............17, 25
Exchequer Gate 226

Fairs 97
Farm of city............. 71, 178

PAGE

Fields, open 37, 191
Fire Fighting services....... 207
Five Burghs 30
Flints 12
Forests, Royal 62
Forum 19, 20
Fossdyke..23, 32, 122, 176, 190, 196
Fosse Way 25
Foster and Co. 202, 203
Freemen 174, 193
Friars, Augustinian 115
— , Black (Dominican).... 113
— , Grey (Franciscan) 110
— , White (Carmelite) 114
—   of the Sack 114

Gainas.................... 28
Gaius, Julius Galenus 16
Gas supply 208
Gaunt, John of........ 56-58, 179
— , —   Palace 57
— , —   Stables..... 96
George Hotel 68
Ghetto 79
Gilbert d'Umfraville 119
Gild Merchant 71
— , St. Anne's 93
— , St. Mary's 94, 95
— , Weaver's 89, 90
Gilds, Craft 88, 91
— , Religious 93
Government of city..70-76, 167-180
Grammar School 156
Greestone Stairs 227
Guildhall................172, 224
—   Street 33

Hannah, John.............. 152
Health Services 211
Heneage, Dean...........131, 223
Hengist 27
Henry II..............47, 58, 89
—   III............ 53, 83, 95
—   VI 63
— ..VII 63
—   VIII 64, 124, 130

PAGE

High Bridge 131
— — Chapel 131
Highways, care of 163
Holmes Common 175, 193
Hospital, Christ's........... 158
— , General........... 188
— , Holy Innocents 116
— , Holy Sepulchre 118
— , St. Bartholomew's.. 119
— , St. Giles' 118, 119
— , St. Leonard's 119
Housing 205, 210
Howard, Catherine 64
— , John 165
— , Lord 185
Hudson, George 199
Hugh, Little St. 81
Hussey, Lord 127
Hutchinson, John 109

Insignia 178

James I 67, 109
— II 150
Jersey School 112, 162
Jews 77-84
Jews' Court................ 79
— House 79, 84
John, King............ 39, 50, 59
Jopin 81

Lawmen 34, 38, 70
Legion, Ninth 15
— , Sixth 16
Leprosy 116
Lincoln, Derivation of name..14, 16
Lindum 14
Lincolnshire Rising 124
Lindiswaras 28
Littleborough 16
Long-and-short work 135
Louis of France 40
Louth 125
Lucy Tower (Castle) 220
— — (Brayford) 33, 220
Lytherland, Harry 131

PAGE

Maces 178
Maddison, Sir Edward 125
Magazine House 141, 142
Magistrates 173
Magna Carta.............. 40
Malandry (see Hospital, Holy
Innocents') 115
Markets 97
Marshall, William 142
Massey-Mainwaring, The
Hon. W. F............... 106
Matilda 38, 39
Mayor's Office 70, 170
Mechanics' Institute 112
Mercia 28, 30
Methodism 150
Mint 34
Mint Wall................ 20
Miracle Plays 94
Moigne, Thomas 125
Monks' Abbey 104
— Leys 175, 193
Monson, Robert............ 157
Morrice, Abraham 150
Municipal Corporations Act
177, 185

National School 154
Nettleham, Bishop's Manor
House 66, 131
Newland Gate 33
Newport 36
— Arch..............19, 41
Nonconformists 147

Observatory Tower 222
Oliver de Barton 179

Parliaments at Lincoln 61, 114
Paulinus 28
Pensions of priests 109, 133
Pillory 164
Pipe Line, Roman 20
Poor Law 160
Population 34, 121, 187, 204
Pottergate Arch 227

	PAGE
Priory Gate	227
Prisons	148, 165, 225
Puritans	147
Purefoy	142
Quakers	148
Railways	198
Reformation, Effects in Lincoln	130
Religious Houses	103
— Persecution	127
Reyner, Edward	148
Richard I	39, 49, 79
— II	63, 87
— III	100
— de Ravenser	119
— , Earl of Cornwall	81, 82
Robey and Co.	202
Roman canals	23
— Lincoln	15
— milestones	21, 24
— moat	19, 22
— pillar bases	20
— roads	21
— tombstone	15, 16
— walls	19
— west gate	22
Rowena	27
Ruston, Joseph	202
St. Austin's Church	29
— Benedict's Church	133, 135, 148
— Catherine's Priory	67, 106
— Cuthbert's Church	29
— Edmund's Church	29
— Lawrence's Church	29
— Martin's Church	29
— Mary-le-Wigford's Church	135
— Nicholas' Church	36
— Paul's Church	28, 29, 135
— Peter-at-Arches Church	148
— Peter in Eastgate Church	29, 162
— Peter at Gowts Church	135
— Rumbold's Church	29

	PAGE
Saltergate	33
Salter's Lane	22
Saracen's Head	128
Saxon raids	26
Sheriff	38, 61, 71, 168
Shuttleworth, Joseph	201
Silver pennies	34
Sincil Dyke	23, 32
Smith, John	147
— , Richard	158
Social Services	204
Spread Eagle	68
Stamp End	23
Staple	10, 85
Steam packets	196
Stephen, King	39, 58
Stocks	164
Stonebow	22, 173, 224
Stow	50
Stuff Ball	91
Swegn	30
Sword	63
Swynford, Katharine	58
Swine Green	106, 175, 192
Tattershall Chantry	133
Templars, Trial of	54-56
Thornbridge	22
Till Bridge Lane	17
Torksey	24, 29, 57
Trackway, ancient	12
Transport	193, 208
Trent	23, 32, 144
Turnpike roads	194
Unemployment	211
Union of Parishes	134
Ulviet	36
Victoria Infant School	155
Villas, Roman	17
Vortigern	27
Vortimer	27
Waddington	121
Walls	22, 33, 181

PAGE

Wards 70
Warwick, Earl of 58
Water supply 20, 206
Wesleyan movement 150
West, Commodore.......... 196

Westmorland, Joan, Countess
of..................... 58
West Gate................ 41
Whalley, Major General 145
Wigford.................. 32
William I 35, 70
— III 68

PAGE

William of Scotland 50
— the Marshall........ 40
Willoughby of Parham, Lord 139
Winceby 143
Witham, river........ 32, 122, 196
— , Somerset.......... 47
Wool, smuggling 73
— trade 85, 90
Works Chantry............. 132
Wren, Sir Christopher 224

York 16, 104

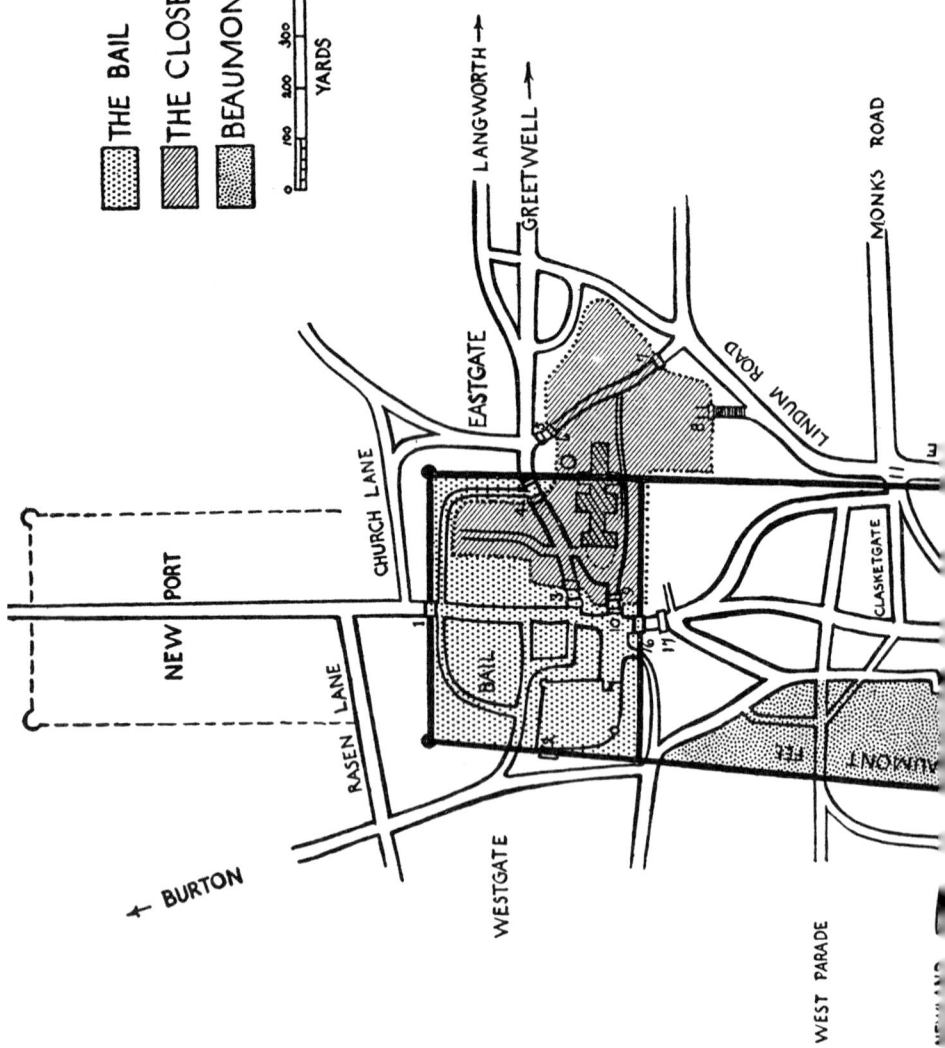

THE BAIL
THE CLOSE
BEAUMONT FEE

YARDS
0 100 200 300 400 500

BURTON →

NEW PORT

RASEN LANE

CHURCH LANE

WESTGATE

EASTGATE

LANGWORTH →

GREETWELL →

LINDUM ROAD

MONKS ROAD

CLASKETGATE

BEAUMONT FEE

WEST PARADE

ROMAN WALLS
..... CLOSE WALL
---- MEDIEVAL CITY DEFENCES

1 NEWPORT ARCH
2 ROMAN WEST GATE
3&4 FOUR GATEHOUSES IN EASTGATE
5 OUTER NORTH GATE
6 INNER NORTH GATE : OLD REGISTRY : PRIORY ARCH
7 POTTERGATE
8 POSTERN ON GREESTONE STAIRS
9 EXCHEQUERGATE
10 MAGAZINE HOUSE
11 CLASKETGATE GATEHOUSE
12 STONEBOW
13 NEWLAND GATE
14 BARGATE (WEST OR GREAT)
15 BARGATE (EAST OR LITTLE)
16 ROMAN SOUTH GATE
17 BAIL GATE
18 TOWER & GATE

BRAYFORD

SINCIL DYKE

ST MARY LE WIGFORD

ST. PETER AT GOWTS

WITHAM

WIGFORD

GREAT GOWT

LITTLE GOWT

15

14